Table of Contents

Snacks on the Go

Funny Face Sandwich Melts

2 super-size English muffins, split and toasted
8 teaspoons *French's*® Sweet & Tangy Honey Mustard
1 can (8 ounces) crushed pineapple, drained
8 ounces sliced smoked ham
4 slices Swiss cheese or white American cheese

1. Place English muffins, cut side up, on baking sheet. Spread each with *2 teaspoons* mustard. Arrange one-fourth of the pineapple, ham and cheese on top, dividing evenly.

2. Broil until cheese melts, about 1 minute. Decorate with mustard and assorted vegetables to create your own funny face. *Makes 4 servings*

Tip: This sandwich is also easy to prepare in the toaster oven.

Prep Time: 10 minutes
Cook Time: 1 minute

How do you make a strawberry shake?

Answer: Take it to a scary movie!

Hot Dog Burritos

1 can (16 ounces) pork and beans
⅓ cup ketchup
2 tablespoons *French's*® Classic Yellow® Mustard
2 tablespoons brown sugar
8 frankfurters, cooked
8 (8-inch) flour tortillas, heated

1. Combine beans, ketchup, mustard and brown sugar in medium saucepan. Bring to boiling over medium-high heat. Reduce heat to low and simmer 2 minutes.

2. Arrange frankfurters in heated tortillas and top with bean mixture. Roll up jelly-roll style.

Makes 8 servings

Tip: Try topping hot dogs with ***French's***® French Fried Onions before rolling up!

Prep Time: 5 minutes
Cook Time: 8 minutes

Kool-Pop Treat

1 (3-ounce) bag ORVILLE REDENBACHER'S® Microwave Popping Corn, popped according to package directions
2 cups brightly colored puffed oat cereal, such as fruit flavored loops
2 cups miniature marshmallows
1 (0.35-ounce) package strawberry soft drink mix
2 tablespoons powdered sugar

1. In large bowl, combine popcorn, cereal and marshmallows.

2. Combine drink mix and powdered sugar; sift over popcorn mixture. Toss to coat.

Makes 12 (1-cup) servings

Hot Dog Burrito

Bread Pudding Snacks

1¼ cups reduced-fat (2%) milk
½ cup cholesterol-free egg substitute
⅓ cup sugar
1 teaspoon vanilla
⅛ teaspoon salt
⅛ teaspoon ground nutmeg (optional)
4 cups ½-inch cinnamon or cinnamon-raisin bread cubes (about 6 bread slices)
1 tablespoon margarine or butter, melted

1. Combine milk, egg substitute, sugar, vanilla, salt and nutmeg, if desired, in medium bowl; mix well. Add bread; mix until well moistened. Let stand at room temperature 15 minutes.

2. Preheat oven to 350°F. Line 12 medium-size muffin cups with paper liners.

3. Spoon bread mixture evenly into prepared cups; drizzle evenly with margarine.

4. Bake 30 to 35 minutes or until snacks are puffed and golden brown. Remove to wire rack to cool completely. *Makes 12 servings*

Note: Snacks will puff up in the oven and fall slightly upon cooling.

Kids' Wrap

- 4 teaspoons honey-Dijon mustard
- 2 (8-inch) fat-free flour tortillas
- 2 slices reduced-fat American cheese, torn into halves
- 4 ounces fat-free oven-roasted turkey breast
- ½ cup shredded carrots (about 1 medium)
- 3 romaine lettuce leaves, washed and torn into bite-size pieces

1. Spread 2 teaspoons mustard evenly over 1 tortilla.

2. Top with 2 cheese halves, half of turkey, half of shredded carrots and half of torn lettuce.

3. Roll up tortilla and cut in half. Repeat with remaining ingredients.

Makes 2 servings

Snackin' Cinnamon Popcorn

- 3 to 4 teaspoons brown sugar substitute
- 1½ teaspoons salt
- 1½ teaspoons ground cinnamon
- 8 cups hot air-popped popcorn
- Butter-flavored nonstick cooking spray

1. Combine brown sugar substitute, salt and cinnamon in small bowl; mix well.

2. Spread hot popped popcorn onto jelly-roll pan; coat with cooking spray and immediately sprinkle cinnamon mixture over popcorn. Serve immediately or store in container at room temperature up to 2 days.

Makes 4 servings (2 cups each)

Kids' Wrap

Monster Sandwiches

8 assorted round and oblong sandwich rolls
Butter or reduced-fat mayonnaise
16 to 24 slices assorted cold cuts (salami, turkey, ham, bologna)
6 to 8 slices assorted cheeses (American, Swiss, Muenster)
1 firm tomato, sliced
1 cucumber, sliced thinly
Assorted lettuce leaves (Romaine, curly, red leaf)
Cocktail onions
Green and black olives
Cherry tomatoes
Pickled gherkins
Radishes
Baby corn
Hard-cooked eggs

1. Cut rolls open just below center and spread with butter.

2. Layer meats, cheeses, tomato and cucumber slices and greens to make monster faces. Roll "tongues" from ham slices or make "lips" with tomato slices.

3. Use toothpicks to affix remaining ingredients for eyes, ears, fins, horns, hair, etc.

Makes 8 sandwiches

Super Suggestion!

Remember to remove toothpicks before eating.

Monster Sandwich

Easy Nachos

4 (6-inch) flour tortillas
Nonstick cooking spray
4 ounces ground turkey
⅔ cup salsa (mild or medium)
2 tablespoons sliced green onion
½ cup (2 ounces) shredded reduced-fat Cheddar cheese

1. Preheat oven to 350°F. Cut each tortilla into 8 wedges; lightly spray one side of wedges with cooking spray. Place on ungreased baking sheet. Bake 5 to 9 minutes or until lightly browned and crisp.

2. Cook ground turkey in small nonstick skillet until browned, stirring with spoon to break up meat. Drain fat. Stir in salsa. Cook until hot.

3. Sprinkle meat mixture over tortilla wedges. Sprinkle with green onion. Top with cheese. Return to oven 1 to 2 minutes or until cheese melts.

Makes 4 servings

Serving Suggestion: Cut tortillas into shapes with cookie cutters and bake as directed.

Note: In a hurry? Substitute baked corn chips for flour tortillas and cooking spray. Proceed as directed.

Fruit and Oat Squares

1 cup all-purpose flour
1 cup uncooked quick oats
¾ cup packed light brown sugar
½ teaspoon baking soda
¼ teaspoon salt
¼ teaspoon ground cinnamon
⅓ cup margarine or butter, melted
¾ cup apricot, cherry or other fruit flavor preserves

1. Preheat oven to 350°F. Spray 9-inch square baking pan with nonstick cooking spray; set aside.

2. Combine flour, oats, brown sugar, baking soda, salt and cinnamon in medium bowl; mix well. Add margarine; stir with fork until mixture is crumbly. Reserve ¾ cup crumb mixture for topping. Press remaining crumb mixture evenly onto bottom of prepared pan. Bake 5 to 7 minutes or until lightly browned. Spread preserves onto crust; sprinkle with reserved crumb mixture.

3. Bake 20 to 25 minutes or until golden brown. Cool completely in pan on wire rack. Cut into 16 squares. *Makes 16 servings*

Tip: Store individually wrapped Fruit and Oat Squares at room temperature up to 3 days or freeze up to 1 month.

Sassy Southwestern Veggie Wraps

½ cup diced zucchini
½ cup diced red or yellow bell pepper
½ cup frozen corn, thawed
1 jalapeño pepper,* seeded and chopped (optional)
¾ cup shredded reduced-fat Mexican cheese blend
3 tablespoons prepared salsa or picante sauce
2 (8-inch) fat-free flour tortillas

**Jalapeño peppers can sting and irritate the skin; wear rubber gloves when handling peppers and do not touch eyes. Wash hands after handling peppers.*

1. Combine zucchini, bell pepper, corn and jalapeño pepper, if desired, in small bowl. Stir in cheese and salsa; mix well.

2. Soften tortillas according to package directions. Spoon vegetable mixture down center of tortillas, distributing evenly; roll up burrito-style. Serve wraps cold or warm.** *Makes 2 servings*

***To warm each wrap, cover loosely with plastic wrap and microwave at HIGH 40 to 45 seconds or until cheese is melted.*

What do you call a carrot who talks back to a farmer?

Answer: A fresh vegetable!

Double-Sauced Chicken Pizza Bagels

1 whole bagel (about 3½ ounces), split in half
4 tablespoons prepared pizza sauce
½ cup diced cooked chicken breast
¼ cup (1 ounce) shredded part-skim mozzarella cheese
2 teaspoons grated Parmesan cheese

1. Place bagel halves on microwavable plate.

2. Spoon 1 tablespoon pizza sauce onto each bagel half. Spread evenly using back of spoon.

3. Top each bagel half with ¼ cup chicken. Spoon 1 tablespoon pizza sauce over chicken on each bagel half. Sprinkle 2 tablespoons mozzarella cheese over top of each bagel half.

4. Cover bagel halves loosely with waxed paper and microwave at HIGH 1 to 1½ minutes or until cheese melts.

5. Carefully remove waxed paper. Sprinkle each bagel half with 1 teaspoon Parmesan cheese. Let stand 1 minute, to cool slightly, before eating. (Bagels will be very hot.) *Makes 2 servings*

Tip: For crunchier "pizzas," toast bagels before adding toppings.

Surfin' Salmon

- ⅓ cup cornflake crumbs
- ⅓ cup cholesterol-free egg substitute
- 2 tablespoons fat-free (skim) milk
- ¾ teaspoon dried dill weed
- ⅛ teaspoon black pepper
- Dash hot pepper sauce
- 1 (14½-ounce) can salmon, drained and skin and bones removed
- Nonstick cooking spray
- 1 teaspoon olive oil
- 6 tablespoons purchased tartar sauce
- 5 small pieces pimiento

1. Stir together cornflake crumbs, egg substitute, milk, dill weed, black pepper and hot pepper sauce in large mixing bowl. Add salmon; mix well.
2. Spray large nonstick skillet with cooking spray. Shape salmon mixture into 5 large egg-shaped balls. Flatten each into ¾-inch-thick oval. Pinch one end of each oval into tail shape for fish.
3. Cook in skillet over medium-high heat 2 to 3 minutes or until lightly browned; turn. Add oil to skillet. Continue cooking 2 to 3 minutes or until firm and lightly browned.
4. Place small drop tartar sauce and pimiento on each for "eye." Serve with remaining tartar sauce, if desired. *Makes 5 servings*

Tip: Serve romaine lettuce on the side of the Surfin' Salmon patty to add the look of sea plants. What a fun way to get your little one to eat fresh vegetables!

Creamy Strawberry-Orange Pops

1 container (8 ounces) strawberry-flavored yogurt
¾ cup orange juice
2 teaspoons vanilla
2 cups frozen whole strawberries
2 teaspoons sugar substitute
6 (7-ounce) paper cups

1. Combine yogurt, orange juice and vanilla in food processor or blender. Cover and blend until smooth. Add frozen strawberries and sugar substitute. Blend until smooth.

2. Pour into 6 paper cups, filling each about ¾ full. Freeze 1 hour. Insert wooden stick into center of each. Freeze completely. Peel cups to serve.

Makes 6 servings

Dreamy Orange Cheesecake Dip

1 package (8 ounces) reduced-fat cream cheese, softened
½ cup orange marmalade
½ teaspoon vanilla
Grated orange peel (optional)
Mint leaves (optional)
2 cups whole strawberries
2 cups cantaloupe chunks
2 cups apple slices

1. Combine cream cheese, marmalade and vanilla in small bowl; mix well. Garnish with orange peel and mint leaves, if desired.

2. Serve with fruit dippers. *Makes 12 servings*

Note: Dip may be prepared ahead of time. Store, covered, in refrigerator for up to 2 days.

Frozen Fudge Pops

½ cup nonfat sweetened condensed milk
¼ cup unsweetened cocoa powder
1¼ cups nonfat evaporated milk
1 teaspoon vanilla

1. Beat together sweetened condensed milk and cocoa in medium bowl. Add evaporated milk and vanilla; beat until smooth.

2. Pour mixture into 8 small paper cups or 8 popsicle molds. Freeze about 2 hours or until beginning to set. Insert wooden popsicle sticks; freeze solid. *Makes 8 servings*

Peanut Pitas

1 package (8 ounces) small pita breads, cut crosswise in half
16 teaspoons reduced-fat peanut butter
16 teaspoons strawberry fruit spread
1 large banana, peeled and thinly sliced (about 48 slices)

1. Spread inside of each pita half with 1 teaspoon each peanut butter and fruit spread.
2. Fill pita halves evenly with banana slices. Serve immediately.

Makes 8 servings

Honey Bees: Substitute honey for fruit spread.

Jolly Jellies: Substitute any flavor jelly for fruit spread and thin apple slices for banana slices.

P. B. Crunchers: Substitute reduced-fat mayonnaise for fruit spread and celery slices for banana slices.

Banana Tot Pops

3 firm, medium DOLE® Bananas
6 large wooden sticks
½ cup raspberry or other flavored yogurt
1 jar (1¾ ounces) chocolate or rainbow sprinkles

- Cut each banana crosswise in half. Insert wooden stick into each half.
- Pour yogurt into small bowl. Hold banana pop over bowl; spoon yogurt to cover all sides of banana. Allow excess yogurt to drip into bowl. Sprinkle candies over yogurt.
- Place pops on wax paper-lined tray. Freeze 2 hours.

Makes 6 servings

Prep Time: 20 minutes
Freeze Time: 2 hours

Cinnamon-Raisin Roll-Ups

4 ounces reduced-fat cream cheese, softened
½ cup shredded carrots
¼ cup golden raisins
1 tablespoon honey
¼ teaspoon ground cinnamon
4 (7- to 8-inch) whole wheat or regular flour tortillas
8 thin apple wedges (optional)

1. Combine cream cheese, carrots, raisins, honey and cinnamon in small bowl; mix well.

2. Spread tortillas evenly with cream cheese mixture, leaving ½-inch border around edge of each tortilla. Place 2 apple wedges down center of each tortilla; roll up. Wrap in plastic wrap. Refrigerate until ready to serve or pack in lunch box. *Makes 4 servings*

Tip: For extra convenience, prepare roll-ups the night before. In the morning, pack the roll-up in a lunch box along with a frozen juice box. The juice box will be thawed by lunchtime and will keep the snack cold in the meantime!

Peanut Butter-Pineapple Celery Sticks

½ cup low-fat (1%) cottage cheese
½ cup reduced-fat peanut butter
½ cup crushed pineapple in juice, drained
12 (3-inch-long) celery sticks

Combine cottage cheese and peanut butter in food processor. Blend until smooth. Stir in pineapple. Stuff celery sticks with mixture.

Makes 6 servings

Serving Suggestion: Substitute 2 medium apples, sliced, for celery.

Cinnamon-Raisin Roll-Ups

Finger Lickin' Chicken Salad

½ cup cubed roasted boneless skinless chicken breast
½ rib celery, cut into 1-inch pieces
¼ cup drained mandarin orange segments
¼ cup red seedless grapes
2 tablespoons fat-free lemon yogurt
1 tablespoon reduced-fat mayonnaise
¼ teaspoon reduced-sodium soy sauce
⅛ teaspoon pumpkin pie spice or ground cinnamon

1. Toss together chicken, celery, oranges and grapes. Place in covered plastic container.
2. For dipping sauce, stir together yogurt, mayonnaise, soy sauce and pumpkin pie spice.
3. Pack chicken mixture and dipping sauce in insulated bag with ice pack. To serve, dip chicken mixture into dipping sauce.

Makes 1 serving

Tip: Alternately thread the chicken, celery, oranges and grapes on wooden skewers for a creative variation to this recipe.

Sloppy Joe's Bun Buggy

4 hot dog buns (not split)
16 thin slices cucumber or zucchini
24 thin strips julienned carrots, 1 inch long
4 ripe olives or pimiento-stuffed olives
Nonstick cooking spray
1 (10-ounce) package extra-lean ground turkey
1¼ cups bottled reduced-fat spaghetti sauce
½ cup chopped broccoli stems
2 teaspoons prepared mustard
½ teaspoon Worcestershire sauce
Dash salt
Dash black pepper
4 small pretzel twists

1. Hollow out hot dog buns. Use wooden pick to make four holes in sides of each bun to attach "wheels." Use wooden pick to make one hole in center of each cucumber slice; push carrot strip through hole. Press into holes in buns, making "wheels" on buns.

2. Cut each olive in half horizontally. Use wooden pick to make two holes in one end of each bun to attach "headlights." Use carrot strips to attach olives to buns, making "headlights."

3. Spray large nonstick skillet with cooking spray. Cook turkey in skillet over medium heat until no longer pink. Stir in spaghetti sauce, broccoli stems, mustard, Worcestershire, salt and pepper; heat through.

4. Spoon sauce mixture into hollowed-out buns. Press pretzel twist into ground turkey mixture, making "windshield" on each buggy.

Makes 4 servings

One Potato, Two Potato

Nonstick cooking spray
2 medium baking potatoes, cut lengthwise into 4 wedges
Salt
½ cup plain dry bread crumbs
2 tablespoons grated Parmesan cheese (optional)
1½ teaspoons dried oregano leaves, dill weed, Italian herbs or paprika
Spicy brown or honey mustard, ketchup or reduced-fat sour cream

1. Preheat oven to 425°F. Spray baking sheet with nonstick cooking spray; set aside.

2. Spray cut sides of potatoes generously with cooking spray; sprinkle lightly with salt.

3. Combine bread crumbs, Parmesan cheese and desired herb in shallow dish. Add potatoes; toss lightly until potatoes are generously coated with crumb mixture. Place on prepared baking sheet.

4. Bake potatoes until browned and tender, about 20 minutes. Serve warm as dippers with mustard.

Makes 4 servings

Potato Sweets: Omit Parmesan cheese, herbs and mustard. Substitute sweet potatoes for baking potatoes. Cut and spray potatoes as directed; coat generously with desired amount of cinnamon-sugar. Bake as directed. Serve warm as dippers with peach or pineapple preserves or honey mustard.

What kind of toes do people like to eat?

Answer: Tomatoes and potatoes.

Little Piggy Pies

2 cups frozen mixed soup vegetables (carrots, potatoes, peas, celery, green beans, corn, onions and lima beans)
1 (10¾-ounce) can reduced-fat condensed cream of chicken soup, undiluted
8 ounces chopped cooked chicken
⅓ cup plain low-fat yogurt
⅓ cup water
½ teaspoon dried thyme leaves
¼ teaspoon poultry seasoning or ground sage
⅛ teaspoon garlic powder
1 (7½-ounce) package refrigerated buttermilk biscuits (10 biscuits)

1. Preheat oven to 400°F.

2. Remove 10 green peas from frozen mixed vegetables; set aside. Stir together remaining frozen vegetables, soup, chicken, yogurt, water, thyme, poultry seasoning and garlic powder in medium saucepan. Bring to a boil, stirring frequently. Cover; keep warm.

3. Press five biscuits into 3-inch circles. Cut each remaining biscuit into eight wedges. Place two wedges on top of each circle; fold points down to form ears. Roll one wedge into small ball; place in center of each circle to form pig's snout. Use tip of spoon handle to make indents in snout for nostrils. Place 2 reserved green peas on each circle for eyes.

4. Spoon hot chicken mixture into 5 (10-ounce) custard cups. Place one biscuit "pig" on top of each. Place remaining biscuit wedges around each "pig" on top of chicken mixture, twisting one wedge "tail" for each. Bake 9 to 11 minutes or until biscuits are golden. *Makes 5 servings*

Prep Time: 10 minutes
Bake Time: 11 minutes

Little Piggy Pie

Confetti Tuna in Celery Sticks

1 (3-ounce) pouch of STARKIST® Premium Albacore or Chunk Light Tuna
½ cup shredded red or green cabbage
½ cup shredded carrot
¼ cup shredded yellow squash or zucchini
3 tablespoons reduced-calorie cream cheese, softened
1 tablespoon plain low-fat yogurt
½ teaspoon dried basil, crushed
Salt and pepper to taste
10 to 12 (4-inch) celery sticks, with leaves if desired

1. In a small bowl toss together tuna, cabbage, carrot and squash.
2. Stir in cream cheese, yogurt and basil. Add salt and pepper to taste.
3. With small spatula spread mixture evenly into celery sticks.

Makes 10 to 12 servings

Tuna Schooners

2 (3-ounce) cans water-packed light tuna, drained
½ cup finely chopped apple
¼ cup shredded carrot
⅓ cup reduced-fat ranch salad dressing
2 English muffins, split and lightly toasted
8 triangular-shaped baked whole wheat crackers or triangular-shaped tortilla chips

1. Combine tuna, apple and carrot in medium bowl. Add salad dressing; stir to combine.
2. Spread ¼ of tuna mixture over top of each muffin half. Stand 2 crackers on each muffin and press firmly into tuna mixture half to form "sails."

Makes 4 servings

Confetti Tuna in Celery Sticks

Peach Freezies

1½ cups (12 ounces) canned or thawed frozen peach slices, drained

¾ cup peach nectar

1 tablespoon sugar

¼ to ½ teaspoon coconut extract (optional)

1. Place peaches, nectar, sugar and extract, if desired, in food processor or blender container; process until smooth.

2. Spoon 2 tablespoons fruit mixture into each section of ice cube trays.*

3. Freeze until almost firm. Insert toothpick into each cube; freeze until firm.

Makes 12 servings

**Or, pour ⅓ cup fruit mixture into each of 8 plastic pop molds or small paper or plastic cups. Freeze until almost firm. Insert wooden stick into each mold; freeze until firm. Makes 8 servings.*

Apricot Freezies: Substitute canned apricot halves for peach slices and apricot nectar for peach nectar.

Pear Freezies: Substitute canned pear slices for peach slices, pear nectar for peach nectar and almond extract for coconut extract.

Pineapple Freezies: Substitute crushed pineapple for peach slices and unsweetened pineapple juice for peach nectar.

Mango Freezies: Substitute chopped fresh mango for canned peach slices and mango nectar for peach nectar. Omit coconut extract.

Peanut Butter & Jelly Shakes

1½ cups vanilla ice cream
¼ cup milk
2 tablespoons creamy peanut butter
6 peanut butter sandwich cookies, coarsely chopped
¼ cup strawberry preserves

1. Place ice cream, milk and peanut butter in blender. Blend on medium speed 1 to 2 minutes or until smooth and well blended. Add chopped cookies and blend 10 seconds on low speed. Pour into 2 serving glasses.

2. Place preserves and 1 to 2 teaspoons water in small bowl; stir until smooth. Stir 2 tablespoons preserve mixture into each shake. Serve immediately.

Makes 2 servings

Serve It With Style: For a change of pace, prepare these shakes using different flavors of preserves.

Cook's Note: Eat this thick and creamy shake with a spoon for a mouthful of cookies in every bite.

Prep Time: 10 minutes

"Moo-vin" Chocolate Milk Shakes

- **1 pint low-fat chocolate ice cream**
- **½ cup fat-free (skim) milk**
- **1 tablespoon chocolate syrup**
- **¼ teaspoon vanilla**
- **⅛ teaspoon decorator sprinkles (optional)**

Combine all ingredients except decorator sprinkles in blender container. Cover and blend until smooth. Pour into 2 small glasses. Add decorator sprinkles, if desired. Serve immediately. *Makes 2 servings*

"Moo-vin" Strawberry Milk Shakes

- **1 pint low-fat vanilla ice cream**
- **1 cup thawed frozen unsweetened strawberries**
- **¼ cup fat-free (skim) milk**
- **¼ teaspoon vanilla**

Combine all ingredients in blender container. Cover and blend until smooth. Pour into 2 small glasses. Serve immediately.

Makes 2 servings

Clockwise from top left: "Moo-vin" Chocolate Milk Shake, "Moo-vin" Vanilla Milk Shake (page 48) and "Moo-vin" Strawberry Milk Shake

Citrus Punch

4 oranges, sectioned
1 to 2 limes, cut into ⅛-inch slices
1 lemon, cut into ⅛-inch slices
1 pint strawberries, stemmed and halved
1 cup raspberries
2 cups orange juice
2 cups grapefruit juice
¾ cup lime juice
½ cup light corn syrup
1 bottle (750 mL) ginger ale or white grape juice
Fresh mint sprigs for garnish

1. Spread oranges, limes, lemon, strawberries and raspberries on baking sheet. Freeze 4 hours or until firm.

2. Combine juices and corn syrup in 2-quart pitcher. Stir until corn syrup dissolves. (Stir in additional corn syrup to taste.) Refrigerate 2 hours or until cold. Stir in ginger ale just before serving.

3. Divide frozen fruit between 8 (12-ounce) glasses. Fill glasses with punch. Garnish with mint springs, if desired. Serve immediately.

Makes 8 to 10 servings (about 5 cups)

Sparkling Apple Punch

2 bottles (750 mL each) sparkling apple cider, chilled
1½ quarts papaya or apricot nectar, chilled
Ice
1 or 2 papayas, peeled and chopped
Orange slices

Combine apple cider, papaya nectar and ice in punch bowl. Add papaya and orange slices. *Makes about 4 quarts*

Top to bottom: Citrus Punch, Sparkling Apple Punch

Banana Smoothies & Pops

1 (14-ounce) can EAGLE BRAND® Sweetened Condensed Milk (NOT evaporated milk)

1 (8-ounce) container vanilla yogurt

2 ripe bananas

½ cup orange juice

1. In blender container, combine all ingredients; blend until smooth. Stop occasionally to scrape down sides.
2. Serve immediately. Store leftovers covered in refrigerator.

Makes 4 cups

Banana Smoothie Pops: Spoon banana mixture into 8 (5-ounce) paper cups. Freeze 30 minutes. Insert wooden craft sticks into the center of each cup; freeze until firm. Makes 8 pops.

Fruit Smoothies: Substitute 1 cup of your favorite fruit and ½ cup any fruit juice for bananas and orange juice.

Prep Time: 5 minutes

"Moo-vin" Vanilla Milk Shakes

1 pint low-fat vanilla ice cream

½ cup fat-free (skim) milk

½ teaspoon vanilla

⅛ teaspoon decorator sprinkles (optional)

Combine all ingredients except decorator sprinkles in blender container. Cover and blend until smooth. Pour into 2 small glasses. Add decorator sprinkles, if desired. Serve immediately. *Makes 2 servings*

Bobbing Head Punch

- Assorted candies
- Assorted fruit slices and pieces
- Water
- 6 cups white grape juice
- 2 cups apple juice or 2 additional cups ginger ale
- 4 cups ginger ale
- Green food coloring

1. Arrange candies and fruit pieces in bottom of 9-inch glass pie plate to create a face. (Remember, the bottom of the face is what will show in the punch bowl.)

2. Add water to cover face and carefully place in freezer. Freeze overnight.

3. At time of serving, combine juice and ginger ale in 4- to 5-quart punch bowl. Tint mixture green. Invert pie plate, placing one hand underneath, and run under cold running water to release frozen face. Place ice mold upside down on top of juice mixture and serve.

Makes 20 cups

Plum Slush

- 6 fresh California plums, halved, pitted and coarsely chopped
- 1 can (6 ounces) frozen cranberry juice concentrate
- 20 ice cubes, cracked

Add plums, juice concentrate and ice cubes to food processor or blender. Process until smooth. Serve immediately. *Makes 8 servings*

Favorite recipe from **California Tree Fruit Agreement**

Bobbing Head Punch

Purple Cow Jumped Over the Moon

3 cups vanilla frozen yogurt
1 cup reduced-fat (2%) milk
½ cup thawed frozen grape juice concentrate (undiluted)
1½ teaspoons lemon juice

Place yogurt, milk, grape juice concentrate and lemon juice in food processor or blender container; process until smooth. Serve immediately.

Makes 8 (½-cup) servings

Razzmatazz Shake: Place 1 quart vanilla frozen yogurt, 1 cup vanilla yogurt and ¼ cup chocolate syrup in food processor or blender container; process until smooth. Pour ½ of mixture evenly into 12 glasses; top with ½ of (12-ounce) can root beer. Fill glasses equally with remaining yogurt mixture; top with remaining root beer. Makes 12 (⅔-cup) servings.

Sunshine Shake: Place 1 quart vanilla frozen yogurt, 1⅓ cups orange juice, 1 cup fresh or thawed frozen raspberries and 1 teaspoon sugar in food processor or blender container; process until smooth. Pour into 10 glasses; sprinkle with ground nutmeg. Makes 10 (½-cup) servings.

Fruit 'n Juice Breakfast Shake

1 extra-ripe, medium DOLE® Banana
¾ cup DOLE® Pineapple Juice
½ cup lowfat vanilla yogurt
½ cup blueberries

Combine all ingredients in blender. Blend until smooth.

Makes 2 servings

Party

Shamrock Smoothies

- 1 tablespoon sugar
- 2 green spearmint candy leaves
- 2 thin round chocolate mints or chocolate sandwich cookies
- 1 ripe banana, peeled and cut into chunks
- 1 cup ice cubes
- ¾ cup apple juice
- ¼ cup plain yogurt
- ½ teaspoon vanilla
- ¼ teaspoon orange extract
- 2 to 3 drops green food coloring

1. Place small sheet of waxed paper on work surface; sprinkle with sugar. Place spearmint leaves on waxed paper; top with second sheet of waxed paper. Roll out leaves to ¼-inch thickness. Cut out 2 (1¼×1-inch) shamrock shapes using small knife or scissors. Press 1 shamrock onto each mint; set aside.

2. Place banana, ice cubes, apple juice, yogurt, vanilla, orange extract and food coloring in blender or food processor; blend until smooth and frothy. Pour into glasses. Garnish with mints.

Makes 2 servings (about 8 ounces each)

Sinister Slushies

4 bottles brightly colored sport drinks
4 to 8 ice cube trays

1. Pour sport drinks into separate ice cube trays and freeze overnight.
2. Just before serving, place each color frozen cubes in separate resealable freezer bag, one color at a time. Seal bag and smash cubes with rolling pin.
3. Layer different colored ice slush in clear glasses to make wild combinations.

Makes 4 to 8 servings

Mysterious Chocolate Mint Cooler

2 cups cold whole milk or half-and-half
¼ cup chocolate syrup
1 teaspoon peppermint extract
Crushed ice
Aerosol whipped topping
Mint leaves

Combine first 3 ingredients in small pitcher; stir until well blended. Fill glasses with crushed ice. Pour chocolate mint mixture over ice. Top with whipped topping and garnish with mint leaves.

Makes about 2 (10-ounce) servings

Snowbird Mocktails

3 cups pineapple juice
1 can (14 ounces) sweetened condensed milk
1 can (6 ounces) frozen orange juice concentrate, thawed
½ teaspoon coconut extract
1 bottle (32 ounces) ginger ale, chilled

1. Combine pineapple juice, sweetened condensed milk, orange juice concentrate and coconut extract in large pitcher; stir well. Refrigerate, covered, until ready to serve (up to 1 week).

2. To serve, pour ½ cup pineapple juice mixture into individual glasses (over crushed ice, if desired). Top off each glass with about ⅓ cup ginger ale. *Makes 10 servings*

Prep Time: 10 minutes

Super Suggestion!

Store unopened cans of sweetened condensed milk at room temperature up to 6 months. Once opened, the milk can be stored in an airtight container in the refrigerator for up to 5 days.

Pizza Fondue

- ½ pound bulk Italian sausage
- 1 cup chopped onion
- 2 jars (26 ounces each) meatless pasta sauce
- 4 ounces thinly sliced ham, finely chopped
- 1 package (3 ounces) sliced pepperoni, finely chopped
- ¼ teaspoon red pepper flakes
- 1 pound mozzarella cheese, cut into ¾-inch cubes
- 1 loaf Italian or French bread, cut into 1-inch cubes

Slow Cooker Directions

1. Cook sausage and onion in large skillet until sausage is browned. Drain off fat.

2. Transfer sausage mixture to slow cooker. Stir in pasta sauce, ham, pepperoni and pepper flakes. Cover; cook on LOW 3 to 4 hours.

3. Serve fondue with cheese cubes and bread cubes.

Makes 20 to 25 appetizer servings

Prep Time: 15 minutes
Cook Time: 3 to 4 hours

Corn Dogs

8 hot dogs

8 wooden craft sticks

1 package (about 16 ounces) refrigerated grand-size corn biscuits

⅓ cup *French's*® Classic Yellow® Mustard

8 slices American cheese, cut in half

1. Preheat oven to 350°F. Insert 1 wooden craft stick halfway into each hot dog; set aside.

2. Separate biscuits. On floured board, press or roll each biscuit into a 7×4-inch oval. Spread 2 *teaspoons* mustard lengthwise down center of each biscuit. Top each with 2 pieces of cheese. Place hot dog in center of biscuit. Fold top of dough over end of hot dog. Fold sides towards center, enclosing hot dog. Pinch edges to seal.

3. Place corn dogs, seam-side down, on greased baking sheet. Bake 20 to 25 minutes or until golden brown. Cool slightly before serving.

Makes 8 servings

Tip: Corn dogs may be made without wooden craft sticks.

Prep Time: 15 minutes
Cook Time: 20 minutes

Perfect Pita Pizzas

2 whole wheat or white pita bread rounds
½ cup spaghetti or pizza sauce
¾ cup (3 ounces) shredded part-skim mozzarella cheese
1 small zucchini, sliced ¼ inch thick
½ small carrot, peeled and sliced
2 cherry tomatoes, halved
¼ small green bell pepper, sliced

1. Preheat oven to 375°F. Line baking sheet with foil; set aside.

2. Using small scissors, carefully split each pita bread round around edge; separate to form 2 rounds.

3. Place rounds, rough sides up, on prepared baking sheet. Bake 5 minutes.

4. Spread 2 tablespoons spaghetti sauce onto each round; sprinkle with cheese. Decorate with vegetables to create faces. Bake 10 to 12 minutes or until cheese melts.

Makes 4 servings

Pepperoni Pita Pizzas: Prepare pita rounds, partially bake and top with spaghetti sauce and cheese as directed. Place 2 small pepperoni slices on each pizza for eyes. Decorate with cut-up fresh vegetables for rest of face. Continue to bake as directed.

Why does a Mexican weather report make you hungry?

Answer: Because it's chili today and hot tamale!

Pizza Rollers

1 package (10 ounces) refrigerated pizza dough
½ cup pizza sauce
18 slices turkey pepperoni
6 sticks mozzarella cheese

1. Preheat oven to 425°F. Coat baking sheet with nonstick cooking spray.
2. Roll out pizza dough on baking sheet to form 12×9-inch rectangle. Cut dough into 6 (4½×4-inch) rectangles. Spread about 1 tablespoon sauce over center third of each rectangle. Top with 3 slices pepperoni and 1 stick of mozzarella cheese. Bring ends of dough together over cheese, pinching to seal. Place seam side down on prepared baking sheet.
3. Bake 10 minutes or until golden brown. *Makes 6 servings*

Tortellini Teasers

½ (9-ounce) package refrigerated cheese tortellini
1 large red or green bell pepper, cut into 1-inch pieces
2 medium carrots, peeled and sliced ½ inch thick
1 medium zucchini, sliced ½ inch thick
12 medium fresh mushrooms
12 cherry tomatoes
1 can (15 ounces) tomato sauce

1. Cook tortellini according to package directions; drain.
2. Alternate 1 tortellini and 2 to 3 vegetable pieces on long frilled wooden picks or wooden skewers.
3. Warm tomato sauce in small saucepan. Serve with dippers.

Makes 6 servings

Pizza Rollers

Baseball Sandwich

Ingredients

1 (1-pound) round sourdough or white bread loaf
2 cups mayonnaise or salad dressing, divided
¼ pound thinly sliced roast beef
1 slice (about 1 ounce) provolone or Swiss cheese
3 tablespoons roasted red peppers, well drained
3 tablespoons spicy mustard, divided
¼ pound thinly sliced ham
1 slice (about 1 ounce) Cheddar cheese
3 tablespoons dill pickle slices
2 tablespoons thinly sliced onion
Red food coloring

Supplies

Pastry bag and small writing tip

1. Cut thin slice off top of bread loaf; set aside. With serrated knife, cut around sides of bread, leaving ¼-inch-thick bread shell. Lift out center portion of bread; horizontally cut removed bread round into 3 slices of equal thickness.

2. Spread 1 tablespoon mayonnaise onto bottom of hollowed out loaf; top with layers of roast beef and provolone cheese. Cover with bottom bread slice and red peppers.

3. Spread top of middle bread slice with ½ of mustard; place over peppers. Top with layers of ham and Cheddar cheese. Spread remaining bread slice with remaining mustard; place over ham and Cheddar cheese. Top with pickles and onion. Replace top of bread loaf.

4. Reserve ⅓ cup mayonnaise; set aside. Frost outside of entire loaf of bread with remaining mayonnaise. Color reserved ⅓ cup mayonnaise with red food coloring; spoon into pastry bag fitted with writing tip. Pipe red mayonnaise onto bread to resemble stitches on baseball.

Makes 6 to 8 servings

Surprise Package Cupcakes

- 1 package (18 ounces) chocolate cake mix, plus ingredients to prepare mix
- Food coloring (optional)
- 1 container (16 ounces) vanilla frosting
- 1 tube ($4\frac{1}{4}$ ounces) white decorator icing
- 72 chewy fruit squares, assorted colors
- Assorted round sprinkles and birthday candles

1. Line 24 standard ($2\frac{1}{2}$-inch) muffin cups with paper liners or spray with nonstick cooking spray. Prepare cake mix and bake in prepared muffin cups according to package directions. Cool in pans on wire racks 15 minutes. Remove cupcakes to racks and cool completely.

2. If desired, tint frosting with food coloring, adding a few drops at a time until desired color is reached. Frost cupcakes with white or tinted frosting.

3. Use decorator icing to pipe "ribbons" on fruit squares to resemble wrapped presents. Place 3 candy presents on each cupcake. Decorate with sprinkles and candles as desired.

Makes 24 cupcakes

Colorific Pizza Cookie

1 package (17½ ounces) sugar cookie mix
⅔ cup mini candy-coated chocolate pieces
⅓ cup powdered sugar
2 to 3 teaspoons milk

1. Preheat oven to 375°F.

2. Prepare cookie mix according to package directions. Spread onto ungreased 12-inch pizza pan. Sprinkle evenly with chocolate pieces; press gently into dough.

3. Bake 20 to 24 minutes or until lightly browned. Cool 2 minutes in pan. Transfer to wire rack and cool completely.

4. Blend powdered sugar and milk until smooth, adding enough milk to reach drizzling consistency. Drizzle icing over cooled pizza cookie with spoon or fork. Cut into wedges. *Makes 12 servings*

Hershey®s Syrup Snacking Brownies

½ cup (1 stick) butter or margarine, softened
1 cup sugar
1½ cups (16-ounce can) HERSHEY®S Syrup
4 eggs
1¼ cups all-purpose flour
1 cup HERSHEY®S Semi-Sweet Chocolate Chips

1. Heat oven to 350°F. Grease 13×9×2-inch baking pan.

2. Beat butter and sugar in large bowl. Add syrup, eggs and flour; beat well. Stir in chocolate chips. Pour batter into prepared pan.

3. Bake 30 to 35 minutes or until brownies begin to pull away from sides of pan. Cool completely in pan on wire rack. Cut into bars.

Makes about 36 brownies

Colorific Pizza Cookie

Lazy Daisy Cupcakes

1 package (18 ounces) yellow cake mix, plus ingredients to prepare mix

Food coloring

1 container (16 ounces) vanilla frosting

30 large marshmallows

24 small round candies or gum drops

1. Line 24 standard (2½-inch) muffin cups with paper liners or spray with nonstick cooking spray. Prepare cake mix and bake in prepared muffin cups according to package directions. Cool in pans on wire racks 15 minutes. Remove cupcakes to racks and cool completely.

2. Add food coloring to frosting, a few drops at a time, until desired color is reached. Frost cooled cupcakes with tinted frosting.

3. With scissors, cut each marshmallow crosswise into 4 pieces. Stretch pieces into petal shapes, and place 5 pieces on each cupcake to form a flower. Place candy in center of each flower. *Makes 24 cupcakes*

Why did the strawberry need a lawyer?

Answer: Because it was in a jam!

Lazy Daisy Cupcake

Trick-or-Treat Pizza Biscuits

- 1 can (16 to 17 ounces or 8 biscuits) refrigerated jumbo biscuits
- 3 tablespoons prepared pizza sauce
- Assorted pizza toppings such as pepperoni slices, cooked crumbled Italian sausage, sliced mushrooms and black olives
- ½ cup shredded pizza-blend or mozzarella cheese
- 1 egg yolk
- 1 teaspoon water
- Assorted food colorings

1. Preheat oven to 375°F. Press 4 biscuits into 4-inch rounds on ungreased baking sheet. Spread center of each biscuit with about 2 teaspoons pizza sauce. Place 4 to 5 pepperoni slices or toppings of your choice on each biscuit; top with 2 tablespoons cheese. Press remaining 4 biscuits into 4-inch rounds and place over cheese; press edges together to seal. Press design into top of each biscuit with Halloween cookie cutter, being careful not to cut all the way through top biscuit.

2. Combine egg yolk and water in small bowl. Divide yolk mixture into several small bowls and tint each with food colorings to desired colors. Decorate Halloween imprints with egg yolk paints. Bake 12 to 15 minutes or until biscuits are golden brown at edges.

Makes 4 servings

Note: These biscuits taste best when made with regular biscuits and not butter-flavored biscuits.

Dem Bones

- 1 package (6 ounces) sliced ham
- ¾ cup (3 ounces) shredded Swiss cheese
- ½ cup mayonnaise
- 1 tablespoon sweet pickle relish
- ½ teaspoon yellow mustard
- ¼ teaspoon black pepper
- 6 slices white bread

1. Place ham in bowl of food processor or blender; process until ground. Combine ham, cheese, mayonnaise, relish, mustard and pepper in small bowl until well blended.

2. Cut out 12 bone shapes from bread using 3½-inch bone-shaped cookie cutter or sharp knife. Spread half of "bones" with 2 tablespoons ham mixture; top with remaining "bones." *Makes 6 bone sandwiches*

Grilled Cheese Jack-O-Lanterns

- 3 tablespoons butter or margarine, softened
- 8 slices bread
- 4 slices Monterey Jack cheese
- 4 slices sharp Cheddar cheese

1. Preheat oven to 350°F. Spread butter on 1 side of each bread slice. Place bread buttered-side-down on ungreased cookie sheet. Using small cookie cutters or knife, cut out shapes from 4 bread slices to make jack-o-lantern faces.

2. Layer 1 slice Monterey Jack and 1 slice Cheddar on each of remaining bread slices; bake 10 to 12 minutes or until cheese is melted and bread is toasted. Remove from oven. Place jack-o-lantern bread slices on sandwiches and serve. *Makes 4 servings*

Dem Bones

Creepy Crawler Punch

Creepy Crawler Ice Ring (recipe follows)
2 cups corn syrup
¼ cup water
6 cinnamon sticks
2 tablespoons whole cloves
½ teaspoon ground allspice
2 quarts cranberry juice cocktail
1½ quarts pineapple juice
1 quart orange juice
½ cup lemon juice
2 quarts ginger ale

1. The day or night before serving, prepare Creepy Crawler Ice Ring.
2. Stir together corn syrup and water in medium saucepan over medium-high heat. Add cinnamon sticks, cloves and allspice; stir gently. Bring to a boil and immediately reduce heat to a simmer; simmer 10 minutes.
3. Refrigerate, covered, until chilled. Remove cinnamon sticks and discard. Strain out cloves and discard.
4. In punch bowl, combine syrup mixture with juices and ginger ale. Unmold Creepy Crawler Ice Ring and add to punch bowl.

Makes 36 servings

Creepy Crawler Ice Ring

1 cup gummy worms or other creepy crawler candy
1 quart lemon-lime sports drink

Arrange gummy worms in bottom of 5-cup ring mold; fill mold with sports drink. Freeze until solid, 8 hours or overnight.

Creepy Cookie Cauldrons

- **1 package (18 ounces) refrigerated chocolate cookie dough***
- **All-purpose flour (optional)**
- **1 bag (14 ounces) caramels, wrappers removed**
- **2 tablespoons milk**
- **1 cup crisp rice cereal**
- **¼ cup mini candy-coated chocolate pieces**
- **Black licorice whips and small gummy insects, frogs or lizards**

**If refrigerated chocolate cookie dough is unavailable, add ¼ cup unsweetened cocoa powder to refrigerated sugar cookie dough. Beat in large bowl until well blended.*

1. Grease 36 (1¾-inch) mini muffin cups. Remove dough from wrapper according to package directions. Sprinkle dough with flour to minimize sticking, if necessary.
2. Cut dough into 36 equal pieces; roll into balls. Place 1 ball in bottom of each muffin cup. Press dough onto bottoms and up sides of muffin cups; chill 15 minutes. Preheat oven to 350°F.
3. Bake 8 to 9 minutes. (Cookies will be puffy.) Remove from oven; gently press down center of each cookie with back of spoon. Return to oven 1 minute. Cool cookies in muffin cups 5 minutes. Remove to wire racks; cool completely.
4. Melt caramels and milk in small saucepan over low heat, stirring frequently until smooth. Stir in cereal. Spoon 1 heaping teaspoon caramel mixture into each cookie cup. Immediately sprinkle with mini chocolate pieces.
5. Cut licorice whips into 4½-inch lengths. For each cookie, make small slit in side; insert end of licorice strip. Repeat on other side of cookie to make cauldron handle. Decorate with gummy creatures as desired.

Makes 3 dozen cookies

Haunted Taco Tarts

1 tablespoon vegetable oil
½ cup chopped onion
½ pound ground turkey
1 clove garlic, minced
½ teaspoon dried oregano leaves
½ teaspoon chili powder
¼ teaspoon salt
Egg Yolk Paint (recipe follows)
1 package (15 ounces) refrigerated pie crusts
1 egg white
½ cup chopped tomato
½ cup taco-flavored shredded cheese

1. Heat oil in large skillet over medium heat. Add onion and cook until tender. Add turkey; cook until turkey is no longer pink, stirring occasionally. Stir in garlic, oregano, chili powder and salt; set aside. Preheat oven to 375°F. Lightly grease baking sheets. Prepare Egg Yolk Paint; set aside.

2. On lightly floured surface, roll 1 pie crust to 14-inch diameter. Using 3-inch Halloween cookie cutters, cut out pairs of desired shapes. Repeat with second pie crust, rerolling dough if necessary. Place ½ of shapes on prepared baking sheets. Brush edges with egg white. Spoon about 1 tablespoon taco mixture onto each shape. Sprinkle with 1 teaspoon tomato and 1 teaspoon cheese. Top with remaining matching shapes; press edges to seal. Decorate with Egg Yolk Paint. Bake 10 to 12 minutes or until golden brown. *Makes 14 tarts*

Egg Yolk Paint

4 egg yolks, divided
4 teaspoons water, divided
Red, yellow, blue and green liquid food coloring

Place 1 egg yolk in each of 4 small bowls. Add 1 teaspoon water and few drops different food coloring to each; beat lightly.

Witches' Snack Hats

- 1 package (18 ounces) refrigerated sugar cookie dough
- ¼ cup unsweetened cocoa powder
- 1½ cups semisweet chocolate chips, divided
- 16 sugar ice cream cones
- ⅓ cup butter
- 3 cups dry cereal (mixture of puffed corn, bite-size wheat and toasted oat cereal)
- ½ cup *each* roasted pumpkin seeds and chopped dried cherries or raisins
- 1⅓ cups powdered sugar
- Assorted colored sugars and decors

1. Preheat oven to 350°F. Grease cookie sheets; set aside. Remove dough from wrapper according to package directions. Mix dough and cocoa powder in large bowl until well blended. Shape dough into 16 balls. Flatten each ball on prepared cookie sheet into 3½- to 4-inch circle. Bake 6 to 8 minutes or until set. Cool on cookie sheets 5 minutes; transfer to wire racks to cool completely.

2. Line large tray with waxed paper. Place 1 cup chocolate chips in small microwavable bowl. Microwave on HIGH 1 to 1½ minutes or until melted, stirring at 30-second intervals. Coat sugar cones with chocolate using clean pastry brush. Stand up on prepared tray; let set.

3. Place remaining ½ cup chocolate chips and butter in small microwavable bowl. Microwave on HIGH 1 to 1½ minutes or until melted, stirring at 30-second intervals. Stir well. Place cereal, pumpkin seeds and cherries in large bowl. Pour chocolate mixture over cereal mixture and stir until thoroughly coated. Sprinkle with powdered sugar, ⅓ cup at a time, carefully folding and mixing until thoroughly coated.

4. Fill cone with snack mix. Brush cone edge with additional melted chocolate; attach to center of cookie. Let set. Repeat with remaining cones, snack mix and cookies. Decorate as desired with melted chocolate, colored sugars and decors. *Makes 16 servings*

Hint: To use these hats as place cards, simply write each guest's name on the hat with melted white chocolate, frosting or decorating gel.

Cookie Pizza

1 (18-ounce) package refrigerated sugar cookie dough
2 cups (12 ounces) semi-sweet chocolate chips
1 (14-ounce) can EAGLE BRAND® Sweetened Condensed Milk (NOT evaporated milk)
2 cups candy-coated milk chocolate candies
2 cups miniature marshmallows
½ cup peanuts

1. Preheat oven to 375°F. Press cookie dough into 2 ungreased 12-inch pizza pans. Bake 10 minutes or until golden. Remove from oven.

2. In medium-sized saucepan, melt chips with Eagle Brand. Spread over crusts. Sprinkle with milk chocolate candies, marshmallows and peanuts.

3. Bake 4 minutes or until marshmallows are lightly toasted. Cool. Cut into wedges.

Makes 2 pizzas (24 servings)

Prep Time: 15 minutes
Bake Time: 14 minutes

What did the baby corn say to the mommy corn?

Answer: Where's pop corn?

Chocolate-Caramel S'Mores

12 chocolate wafer cookies or chocolate graham cracker squares

2 tablespoons fat-free caramel topping

6 large marshmallows

1. Prepare coals for grilling. Place 6 wafer cookies top-down on plate. Spread 1 teaspoon caramel topping in center of each wafer to within about ¼ inch of edge.

2. Spear 1 to 2 marshmallows onto long wood-handled skewer.* Hold several inches above coals 3 to 5 minutes or until marshmallows are golden and very soft, turning slowly. Push 1 marshmallow off into center of caramel. Top with plain wafer. Repeat with remaining marshmallows and wafers. *Makes 6 servings*

**If wood-handled skewers are unavailable, use oven mitt to protect hand from heat.*

Note: S'mores, a favorite campfire treat, got their name because everyone who tasted them wanted "some more." In the unlikely event of leftover S'mores, they can be reheated in the microwave on HIGH 15 to 30 seconds.

Mice Creams

1 pint vanilla ice cream

1 (4-ounce) package READY CRUST® Mini-Graham Cracker Pie Crusts

Ears—12 KEEBLER® Grasshopper® cookies

Tails—3 chocolate twigs, broken in half *or* 6 (3-inch) pieces black shoestring licorice

Eyes and noses—18 brown candy-coated chocolate candies

Whiskers—2 teaspoons chocolate sprinkles

Place 1 scoop vanilla ice cream into each crust. Press cookie ears and tails into ice cream. Press eyes, noses and whiskers in place. Serve immediately. Do not refreeze. *Makes 6 servings*

Prep Time: 15 minutes

Polar Bear Banana Bites

1 medium banana, cut into 6 equal-size pieces

¼ cup creamy peanut butter*

3 tablespoons fat-free (skim) milk

¼ cup miniature-size marshmallows

2 tablespoons unsalted dry-roasted peanuts, chopped

1 tablespoon chocolate-flavored decorator sprinkles

**Soy butter or almond butter can be used in place of peanut butter.*

1. Insert wooden pick into each banana piece. Place on tray lined with waxed paper.

2. Whisk together peanut butter and milk. Combine marshmallows, peanuts and chocolate sprinkles in shallow dish. Dip each banana piece in peanut butter mixture, draining off excess. Roll in peanut mixture. Place on tray; let stand until set. *Makes 3 servings*

Mice Creams

Frozen Berry Ice Cream

8 ounces frozen unsweetened strawberries, partially thawed
8 ounces frozen unsweetened peaches, partially thawed
4 ounces frozen unsweetened blueberries, partially thawed
6 packets sugar substitute
2 teaspoons vanilla
2 cups no-sugar-added light vanilla ice cream
16 blueberries
4 small strawberries, halved
8 peach slices

1. In food processor, combine frozen strawberries, peaches, blueberries, sugar substitute and vanilla. Process until coarsely chopped.

2. Add ice cream; process until well blended.

3. Serve immediately for semi-soft texture or freeze until needed and allow to stand 10 minutes to soften slightly before serving. Garnish each serving with 2 blueberries for "eyes," 1 strawberry half for "nose" and 1 peach slice for "smile." *Makes 8 servings (½ cup each)*

Ice Cream Cone Cakes

1 package (18¼ ounces) devil's food cake mix plus ingredients to prepare mix
⅓ cup sour cream
1 package (2⅝ ounces) flat-bottomed ice cream cones (about 18 cones)
1¼ cups frozen yogurt (any flavor)
Cake decorations or chocolate sprinkles

1. Preheat oven to 350°F. Grease and flour 8- or 9-inch round cake pan; set aside.

2. Prepare cake mix according to package directions, substituting sour cream for ⅓ cup of water and decreasing oil to ¼ cup.

3. Spoon ½ of batter (about 2⅓ cups) evenly into ice cream cones, using about 2 tablespoons batter for each. Pour remaining batter into prepared cake pan.

4. Stand cones on cookie sheet. Bake cones and cake layer until toothpick inserted into center of cake comes out clean, about 20 minutes for cones and about 35 minutes for cake layer. Cool on wire racks, removing cake from pan after 10 minutes. Reserve or freeze cake layer for another use.

5. Top each filled cone with ¼ scoop of frozen yogurt just before serving. Sprinkle with decorations as desired. Serve immediately.

Makes 18 servings

Contents

Crunchy Snack Mixes

Find endless combinations of snack mixes kids are sure to love. Fill decorated goodie bags and party cups with these easy-to-serve crunchy treats.

Spicy, Fruity Popcorn Mix

4 cups lightly salted popped popcorn
2 cups corn cereal squares
1½ cups dried pineapple wedges
1 package (6 ounces) dried fruit bits
Butter-flavored nonstick cooking spray
2 tablespoons sugar
1 tablespoon ground cinnamon
1 cup yogurt-covered raisins

1. Preheat oven to 350°F. Combine popcorn, cereal, pineapple and fruit bits in large bowl; mix lightly. Transfer to 15×10-inch jelly-roll pan. Spray mixture generously with cooking spray.

2. Combine sugar and cinnamon in small bowl. Sprinkle half of the sugar mixture over popcorn mixture; toss lightly to coat. Spray mixture again with additional cooking spray. Add remaining sugar mixture; mix lightly.

3. Bake snack mix 10 minutes, stirring after 5 minutes. Cool completely in pan on wire rack. Add raisins; mix lightly. *Makes 7 to 8 cups*

Spicy, Fruity Popcorn Mix

Cinnamon Trail Mix

2 cups corn cereal squares
2 cups whole wheat cereal squares or whole wheat cereal squares with mini graham crackers
1½ cups oyster crackers
½ cup broken sesame snack sticks
2 tablespoons margarine or butter, melted
1 teaspoon ground cinnamon
¼ teaspoon ground nutmeg
½ cup bite-size fruit-flavored candy pieces

1. Preheat oven to 350°F. Spray 13×9-inch baking pan with nonstick cooking spray.

2. Place cereals, oyster crackers and sesame sticks in prepared pan; mix lightly.

3. Combine margarine, cinnamon and nutmeg in small bowl; mix well. Drizzle evenly over cereal mixture; toss to coat.

4. Bake 12 to 14 minutes or until golden brown, stirring gently after 6 minutes. Cool completely. Stir in candies. *Makes 6 cups*

Critter Munch

1½ cups animal cracker cookies
½ (6-ounce) package Cheddar or original flavor fish-shaped crackers (1½ cups)
1 cup dried tart cherries
1 cup candy-coated chocolate candy pieces
1 cup honey-roasted peanuts (optional)

1. Put animal crackers, fish crackers, dried cherries, candy and peanuts, if desired, in a large mixing bowl.

2. Carefully stir with a spoon.

3. Store in a tightly covered container at room temperature.

Makes 5 cups

Favorite recipe from **Cherry Marketing Institute**

Popcorn Crunchies

12 cups popped popcorn (about ¾ cup unpopped)
1½ cups sugar
⅓ cup water
⅓ cup corn syrup
2 tablespoons butter or margarine
1 teaspoon vanilla

1. Preheat oven to 250°F. Grease large shallow roasting pan. Add popcorn. Keep warm in oven while making caramel mixture.

2. Place sugar, water and corn syrup in heavy 2-quart saucepan. Stir over low heat until sugar has dissolved and mixture comes to a boil. Carefully clip candy thermometer to side of pan (do not let bulb touch bottom of pan). Cook over low heat, without stirring, about 10 minutes or until thermometer registers 280°F. Occasionally wash down any sugar crystals that form on side of the pan using pastry brush dipped in warm water. Immediately remove from heat. Stir in butter and vanilla until smooth.

3. Pour hot syrup mixture slowly over warm popcorn, turning to coat kernels evenly. Set aside until cool enough to handle but warm enough to shape. Butter hands. Working quickly, lightly press warm mixture into 2-inch balls. Cool completely. Store in airtight container.

Makes about 14 popcorn balls

Pleasin' Peanutty Snack Mix

- **4 cups whole wheat cereal squares *or* 2 cups whole wheat and 2 cups corn or rice cereal squares**
- **2 cups small pretzel twists or fish-shaped pretzels**
- **½ cup dry-roasted peanuts**
- **2 tablespoons creamy peanut butter**
- **1 tablespoon honey**
- **1 tablespoon apple juice or water**
- **2 teaspoons vanilla**
- **Butter-flavored nonstick cooking spray**
- **½ cup raisins, dried fruit bits or dried cherries (optional)**

1. Preheat oven to 250°F.

2. Combine cereal, pretzels and peanuts in large bowl; set aside.

3. Combine peanut butter, honey and apple juice in small microwavable bowl. Microwave on HIGH 30 seconds or until hot. Stir in vanilla.

4. Drizzle peanut butter mixture evenly over cereal mixture; toss lightly to evenly coat. Place mixture in single layer in ungreased 15×10-inch jelly-roll pan; coat lightly with cooking spray.

5. Bake 8 minutes; stir. Continue baking 8 to 9 minutes or until golden brown. Remove from oven. Add raisins, if desired; mix lightly.

6. Spread mixture in single layer on large sheet of foil to cool.

Makes 6 cups

Make It Special

Add excitement to the party by using empty ice cream cones as individual edible serving bowls for snack mixes. Look for colored cones to add extra pizzazz!

Pleasin' Peanutty Snack Mix

Brontosaurus Bites

4 cups air-popped popcorn
2 cups mini-dinosaur grahams
2 cups corn cereal squares
1½ cups dried pineapple wedges
1 package (6 ounces) dried fruit bits
Butter-flavored nonstick cooking spray
1 tablespoon plus 1½ teaspoons sugar
1½ teaspoons ground cinnamon
½ teaspoon ground nutmeg
1 cup yogurt-covered raisins

1. Preheat oven to 350°F. Combine popcorn, grahams, cereal, pineapple and fruit bits in large bowl; mix lightly. Transfer to 15×10-inch jelly-roll pan. Spray mixture generously with cooking spray.

2. Combine sugar, cinnamon and nutmeg in small bowl. Sprinkle ½ of the sugar mixture over popcorn mixture; toss lightly to coat. Spray mixture again with additional cooking spray. Add remaining sugar mixture; mix lightly.

3. Bake snack mix 10 minutes, stirring after 5 minutes. Cool completely in pan on wire rack. Add raisins; mix lightly. *Makes about 9 cups*

Gorilla Grub: Substitute plain raisins for the yogurt-covered raisins and ¼ cup grated Parmesan cheese for the sugar, cinnamon and nutmeg.

Make It Special

Kids may want to bring snacks home, so be sure to bring small, sturdy paper plates, clear plastic bags and assorted colorful ribbons. Or, you could prepare take-home treats ahead of time. Wrap extra snack mix in festive, colored paper napkins, party bags or small plastic food storage bags decorated with stickers.

Teddy Bear Party Mix

4 cups crisp cinnamon graham cereal
2 cups honey flavored teddy-shaped graham snacks
1 can (1½ ounces) *French's*® Potato Sticks
3 tablespoons melted unsalted butter
2 tablespoons *French's*® Worcestershire Sauce
1 tablespoon packed brown sugar
¼ teaspoon ground cinnamon
1 cup sweetened dried cranberries or raisins
½ cup chocolate, peanut butter or carob chips

1. Preheat oven to 350°F. Lightly spray jelly-roll pan with nonstick cooking spray. Combine cereal, graham snacks and potato sticks in large bowl.

2. Combine butter, Worcestershire, sugar and cinnamon in small bowl; toss with cereal mixture. Transfer to prepared pan. Bake 12 minutes. Cool completely.

3. Stir in dried cranberries and chips. Store in an air-tight container.

Makes about 7 cups

Prep Time: 5 minutes • Cook Time: 12 minutes

Cereal Trail Mix

¼ cup (½ stick) butter or margarine
2 tablespoons sugar
1 teaspoon ground cinnamon
1 cup bite-size oat cereal squares
1 cup bite-size wheat cereal squares
1 cup bite-size rice cereal squares
¼ cup toasted slivered almonds
¾ cup raisins

Melt butter on HIGH 1½ minutes in large microwavable bowl. Add sugar and cinnamon; mix well. Add cereals and nuts; stir to coat. Microwave on HIGH 2 minutes; stir. Microwave 2 minutes more; stir. Add raisins. Microwave an additional 2 to 3 minutes, stirring after 2 minutes. Spread on paper towels; mix will become crisp as it cools. Store tightly covered.

Makes about 4 cups

Birthday Parties

Make birthdays extra special with these fun and sweet decorated treats. Colorful one-of-a-kind cookies, cakes and cupcakes make any party one they're sure to remember.

Dipped, Drizzled & Decorated Pretzels

1 bag chocolate or flavored chips (semisweet, bittersweet, milk chocolate, green mint, white chocolate, butterscotch, peanut butter or a combination)
1 bag pretzel rods
Assorted toppings: jimmies, sprinkles, chopped nuts, coconut, toasted coconut, cookie crumbs, colored sugars

Microwave Directions

1. Place chips in microwavable bowl. (Be sure bowl and utensils are completely dry.) Cover with plastic wrap and turn back one corner to vent. Microwave on HIGH 1 minute; stir. Microwave at 30-second intervals, stirring after each interval, until chips are completely melted. Check and stir frequently.

2. Dip one half of each pretzel rod into melted chocolate and decorate. Roll coated end of several pretzels in toppings. Drizzle others with contrasting color/flavor melted chips. (Drizzle melted chocolate out of spoon while rotating pretzel to get even coverage.)

3. Place decorated pretzels on wire rack set over baking sheet lined with waxed paper. Let coating harden completely. Do not refrigerate.

Makes about 24 pretzels

Cookies & Cream Cupcakes

2¼ cups all-purpose flour
1 tablespoon baking powder
½ teaspoon salt
1⅔ cups sugar
1 cup milk
½ cup (1 stick) butter, softened
2 teaspoons vanilla
3 egg whites
1 cup crushed chocolate sandwich cookies (about 10 cookies) plus additional for garnish
1 container (16 ounces) vanilla frosting

1. Preheat oven to 350°F. Line 24 regular-size (2½-inch) muffin pan cups with paper baking cups.

2. Sift flour, baking powder and salt together in large bowl. Stir in sugar. Add milk, butter and vanilla; beat with electric mixer at low speed 30 seconds. Beat at medium speed 2 minutes. Add egg whites; beat 2 minutes. Stir in 1 cup crushed cookies.

3. Spoon batter into prepared muffin cups. Bake 20 to 25 minutes or until toothpicks inserted into centers come out clean. Cool in pans on wire racks 10 minutes. Remove to racks; cool completely.

4. Frost cupcakes; garnish with additional crushed cookies.

Makes 24 cupcakes

Cookies & Cream Cupcakes

Chocolate Marbled Blondies

½ cup (1 stick) butter or margarine, softened
½ cup firmly packed light brown sugar
1 large egg
2 teaspoons vanilla extract
1½ cups all-purpose flour
1¼ teaspoons baking soda
1 cup "M&M's"® Chocolate Mini Baking Bits, divided
4 ounces cream cheese, softened
2 tablespoons granulated sugar
1 large egg yolk
¼ cup unsweetened cocoa powder

Preheat oven to 350°F. Lightly grease 9×9×2-inch baking pan; set aside. In large bowl cream butter and brown sugar until light and fluffy; beat in egg and vanilla. In medium bowl combine flour and baking soda; blend into creamed mixture. Stir in ⅔ cup "M&M's"® Chocolate Mini Baking Bits; set aside. Dough will be stiff. In separate bowl beat together cream cheese, granulated sugar and egg yolk until smooth; stir in cocoa powder until well blended. Place chocolate-cheese mixture in six equal portions evenly onto bottom of prepared pan. Place reserved dough around cheese mixture and swirl slightly with tines of fork. Pat down evenly on top. Sprinkle with remaining ⅓ cup "M&M's"® Chocolate Mini Baking Bits. Bake 25 to 30 minutes or until toothpick inserted in center comes out with moist crumbs. Cool completely. Cut into bars. Store in refrigerator in tightly covered container. *Makes 16 bars*

Chocolate Marbled Blondies

Banana Split Cupcakes

- 1 package (about 18 ounces) yellow cake mix, divided
- 1 cup water
- 1 cup mashed ripe bananas
- 3 eggs
- 1 cup chopped drained maraschino cherries
- 1½ cups miniature semisweet chocolate chips, divided
- 1½ cups prepared vanilla frosting
- 1 cup marshmallow creme
- 1 teaspoon shortening
- 30 whole maraschino cherries, drained and patted dry

1. Preheat oven to 350°F. Line 30 standard (2½-inch) muffin cups with paper baking cups.

2. Reserve 2 tablespoons cake mix. Combine remaining cake mix, water, bananas and eggs in large bowl. Beat at low speed of electric mixer until moistened, about 30 seconds. Beat at medium speed 2 minutes. Combine chopped cherries and reserved cake mix in small bowl. Stir chopped cherry mixture and 1 cup chocolate chips into batter.

3. Spoon batter into prepared muffin cups. Bake 15 to 20 minutes or until toothpicks inserted into centers come out clean. Cool in pans on wire racks 10 minutes. Remove to wire racks; cool completely.

4. Combine frosting and marshmallow creme in medium bowl until well blended. Frost cupcakes.

5. Combine remaining ½ cup chocolate chips and shortening in small microwavable bowl. Microwave on HIGH 30 to 45 seconds, stirring after 30 seconds, or until smooth. Drizzle chocolate mixture over cupcakes. Place one whole cherry on each cupcake.

Makes 30 cupcakes

Note: Omit chocolate drizzle and top cupcakes with colored sprinkles, if desired.

Reese's® Haystacks

1⅔ cups (10-ounce package) REESE'S® Peanut Butter Chips
1 tablespoon shortening (do *not* use butter, margarine, spread or oil)
2½ cups (5-ounce can) chow mein noodles

1. Line tray with wax paper.

2. Place peanut butter chips and shortening in medium microwave-safe bowl. Microwave at HIGH (100%) 1 minute; stir. If necessary, microwave at HIGH an additional 15 seconds at a time, stirring after each heating, just until chips are melted and mixture is smooth when stirred. Immediately add chow mein noodles; stir to coat.

3. Drop mixture by heaping teaspoons onto prepared tray or into paper candy cups. Let stand until firm. If necessary, cover and refrigerate several minutes until firm. Store in tightly covered container.

Makes about 24 treats

Double Malted Cupcakes

Cupcakes

- **2 cups all-purpose flour**
- **¼ cup malted milk powder**
- **2 teaspoons baking powder**
- **¼ teaspoon salt**
- **1¾ cups granulated sugar**
- **½ cup (1 stick) butter, softened**
- **1 cup reduced-fat (2%) or whole milk**
- **1½ teaspoons vanilla**
- **3 egg whites**

Frosting

- **4 ounces milk chocolate candy bar, broken into chunks**
- **¼ cup (½ stick) butter**
- **¼ cup whipping cream**
- **1 tablespoon malted milk powder**
- **1 teaspoon vanilla**
- **1¾ cups powdered sugar**
- **30 chocolate-covered malted milk balls**

1. Preheat oven to 350°F. Line 30 standard (2½-inch) muffin cups with paper baking cups.

2. For cupcakes, combine flour, ¼ cup malted milk powder, baking powder and salt in medium bowl; mix well and set aside. Beat sugar and ½ cup butter in large bowl with electric mixer at medium speed 1 minute. Add milk and 1½ teaspoons vanilla. Beat at low speed 30 seconds. Gradually beat in flour mixture; beat at medium speed 2 minutes. Add egg whites; beat 1 minute.

3. Spoon batter into prepared muffin cups, filling ⅔ full. Bake 20 minutes or until golden brown and toothpick inserted into centers comes out clean. Cool in pans on wire racks 10 minutes. (Centers of cupcakes will sink slightly upon cooling.) Remove cupcakes to wire racks; cool completely. (At this point, cupcakes may be frozen up to 3 months.)

continued on page 122

Double Malted Cupcakes, continued

4. For frosting, melt chocolate and ¼ cup butter in heavy medium saucepan over low heat, stirring frequently. Stir in cream, 1 tablespoon malted milk powder and 1 teaspoon vanilla; mix well. Gradually stir in powdered sugar. Cook 4 to 5 minutes, stirring constantly, until small lumps disappear. Remove from heat. Refrigerate 20 minutes, beating every 5 minutes or until frosting is spreadable.

5. Spread frosting over cooled cupcakes; decorate with malted milk balls. Store at room temperature up to 24 hours, or cover and refrigerate for up to 3 days before serving. *Makes 30 cupcakes*

Mini Pizza Cookies

1 20-ounce tube refrigerated sugar cookie dough
2 cups (16 ounces) prepared pink frosting
"M&M's"® Chocolate Mini Baking Bits
Variety of additional toppings such as shredded coconut, granola, raisins, nuts, small pretzels, snack mixes, sunflower seeds, popped corn and mini marshmallows

Preheat oven to 350°F. Lightly grease cookie sheets; set aside. Divide dough into 8 equal portions. On lightly floured surface, roll each portion of dough into ¼-inch-thick circle; place circles about 2 inches apart onto prepared cookie sheets. Bake 10 to 13 minutes or until golden brown on edges. Cool completely on wire racks. Spread top of each pizza with frosting; sprinkle with "M&M's"® Chocolate Mini Baking Bits and 2 or 3 suggested toppings. *Makes 8 large cookies*

Chocolate Zucchini Snack Cake

1⅔ cups granulated sugar
½ cup (1 stick) butter, softened
½ cup vegetable oil
2 eggs
1½ teaspoons vanilla
2½ cups all-purpose flour
⅓ cup unsweetened cocoa powder
1 teaspoon baking soda
½ teaspoon salt
½ cup buttermilk
2 cups shredded zucchini
¾ cup chopped pecans (optional)
1 cup semisweet chocolate chips

1. Preheat oven to 325°F. Grease and flour 13×9-inch baking pan.

2. Beat sugar, butter and oil in large bowl with electric mixer at medium speed until well blended.

3. Add eggs, one at a time, beating well after each addition. Blend in vanilla.

4. Combine flour, cocoa, baking soda and salt in medium bowl. Add to butter mixture alternately with buttermilk, beating well after each addition. Stir in zucchini.

5. Pour into prepared pan. Sprinkle with pecans, if desired, and chocolate chips.

6. Bake 55 minutes or until toothpick inserted into center comes out clean. Cool on wire rack. Cut into squares to serve.

Makes 24 squares

Chocolate Zucchini Snack Cake

Red's Rockin' Rainbow Cupcakes

2¼ cups all-purpose flour
1 tablespoon baking powder
½ teaspoon salt
1⅔ cups granulated sugar
½ cup (1 stick) butter, softened
1 cup milk
2 teaspoons vanilla extract
3 large egg whites
Blue and assorted food colorings
1½ cups "M&M's"® Chocolate Mini Baking Bits, divided
1 container (16 ounces) white frosting

Preheat oven to 350°F. Lightly grease 24 (2¾-inch) muffin cups or line with paper or foil liners; set aside. In large bowl combine flour, baking powder and salt. Blend in sugar, butter, milk and vanilla; beat about 2 minutes. Add egg whites; beat 2 minutes. Divide batter evenly among prepared muffin cups. Place 2 drops desired food coloring into each muffin cup. Swirl gently with knife. Sprinkle evenly with ¾ cup "M&M's"® Chocolate Mini Baking Bits. Bake 20 to 25 minutes or until toothpick inserted in centers comes out clean. Cool completely on wire racks. Combine frosting and blue food coloring. Spread frosting over cupcakes; decorate with remaining ¾ cup "M&M's"® Chocolate Mini Baking Bits to make rainbows. Store in tightly covered container.

Makes 24 cupcakes

m

Ultimate Rocky Road Cups

¾ cup (1½ sticks) butter or margarine
4 squares (1 ounce each) unsweetened baking chocolate
1½ cups granulated sugar
3 large eggs
1 cup all-purpose flour
1¾ cups "M&M's"® Chocolate Mini Baking Bits
¾ cup coarsely chopped peanuts (optional)
1 cup mini marshmallows

Preheat oven to 350°F. Generously grease 24 (2½-inch) muffin cups or line with foil liners. Place butter and chocolate in large microwave-safe bowl. Microwave on HIGH 1 minute; stir. Microwave on HIGH an additional 30 seconds; stir until chocolate is completely melted. Add sugar and eggs, one at a time, beating well after each addition; blend in flour. In separate bowl combine "M&M's"® Chocolate Mini Baking Bits and nuts, if desired; stir 1 cup baking bits mixture into brownie batter. Divide batter evenly among prepared muffin cups. Bake 20 minutes. Combine remaining baking bits mixture with marshmallows; divide evenly among muffin cups, topping hot brownies. Return to oven; bake 5 minutes longer. Cool completely before removing from muffin cups. Store in tightly covered container. *Makes 24 cups*

Mini Ultimate Rocky Road Cups: Prepare recipe as directed, dividing batter among 60 generously greased 2-inch mini muffin cups. Bake 15 minutes. Sprinkle with topping mixture; bake 5 minutes longer. Cool completely before removing from cups. Store in tightly covered container. Makes about 60 mini cups.

Ultimate Rocky Road Squares: Prepare recipe as directed, spreading batter into generously greased 13×9×2-inch baking pan. Bake 30 minutes. Sprinkle with topping mixture; bake 5 minutes longer. Cool completely. Cut into squares. Store in tightly covered container. Makes 24 squares.

Novelty Sweets

Journey to the land of make-believe, where simple cakes and cookies are transformed into stunning creations. Kids' eyes will light up with excitement when they discover these whimsical and colorfully decorated sweet treats.

Drum Layer Cake

1 package DUNCAN HINES® Moist Deluxe® Cake Mix (any flavor)
1 container DUNCAN HINES® Creamy Home-Style Classic Vanilla Frosting, divided
Green food coloring
Thin pretzel sticks
Candy-coated chocolate pieces
Lollipops

1. Preheat oven to 350°F. Grease and flour two 8-inch round cake pans.

2. Prepare, bake and cool cake following package directions for basic recipe.

3. To assemble, place half the Vanilla frosting in small bowl. Tint with green food coloring; set aside. Place one cake layer on serving plate. Spread with half of untinted vanilla frosting. Top with second cake layer. Spread green frosting on sides of cake. Spread remaining Vanilla frosting on top of cake. Arrange pretzel sticks and candy-coated chocolates on sides of cake as shown in photograph. Place lollipops on top of cake for "drumsticks." *Makes 12 to 16 servings*

Sunshine Butter Cookies

¾ cup (1½ sticks) butter, softened
¾ cup sugar
1 egg
2¼ cups all-purpose flour
¼ teaspoon salt
Grated peel of ½ lemon
1 teaspoon frozen lemonade concentrate, thawed
Lemonade Royal Icing (page 134)
Thin pretzel sticks
Yellow paste food coloring
Gummy fruit and black licorice strings

1. Beat butter and sugar in large bowl with electric mixer at high speed until fluffy. Add egg; beat well.

2. Combine flour, salt and lemon peel in medium bowl. Add to butter mixture. Stir in lemonade concentrate. Refrigerate 2 hours.

3. Prepare Lemonade Royal Icing. Cover; let stand at room temperature. Preheat oven to 350°F. Grease cookie sheets.

4. Roll dough on floured surface to ⅛-inch thickness. Cut out cookies using 3-inch round cookie cutter. Place cookies on prepared cookie sheets. Press pretzel sticks into edges of cookies to resemble sunshine rays; press gently. Bake 10 minutes or until lightly browned. Remove to wire racks; cool completely.

5. Add food coloring to Lemonade Royal Icing. Spoon about ½ cup icing into resealable food storage bag; seal. Cut tiny tip from corner of bag. Pipe thin circle around flat side of each cookie to create outline.

6. Add water, 1 tablespoon at a time, to remaining icing in bowl until thick but pourable consistency. Spoon icing onto cookie centers, staying within outline.

7. Decorate cookies with gummy fruit and licorice to make sunshine faces. Let stand 1 hour or until dry. *Makes about 3 dozen cookies*

continued on page 134

Sunshine Butter Cookies

Sunshine Butter Cookies, continued

Lemonade Royal Icing

3¾ cups sifted powdered sugar
3 tablespoons meringue powder
6 tablespoons frozen lemonade concentrate, thawed

Beat all ingredients in large bowl with electric mixer at high speed until smooth.

Ghosts on a Stick

4 wooden craft sticks
4 medium pears, stems removed
9 squares (2 ounces each) almond bark
Mini chocolate chips

1. Line baking sheet with waxed paper and 4 paper baking cups. Insert wooden sticks into stem ends of pears.

2. Melt almond bark according to package directions.

3. Dip one pear into melted almond bark, spooning bark over top to coat evenly. Remove excess by scraping pear bottom across rim of measuring cup. Place on paper baking cup; let set 1 minute.

4. Decorate with mini chocolate chips to make ghost face. Repeat with remaining pears.

5. Place spoonful of extra almond bark at bottom of pears for ghost tails. Refrigerate until firm. *Makes 4 servings*

ABC Cookies

½ cup (1 stick) butter, softened
½ cup granulated sugar
1 large egg
2 tablespoons orange juice
1½ cups all-purpose flour
1 teaspoon grated orange peel
½ teaspoon baking powder
⅛ teaspoon salt
Orange Icing (recipe follows)
1 cup "M&M's"® Chocolate Mini Baking Bits

In large bowl cream butter and sugar until light and fluffy; beat in egg and orange juice. In medium bowl combine flour, orange peel, baking powder and salt; add to creamed mixture. Wrap and refrigerate dough 2 to 3 hours. Preheat oven to 350°F. Working with half the dough at a time on well-floured surface, roll to ¼-inch thickness. Cut into letter shapes using 1½-inch cookie cutters. Place about 2 inches apart on ungreased cookie sheets. Bake 8 to 10 minutes. Cool 1 minute on cookie sheets; cool completely on wire racks. Prepare Orange Icing; spread over cookies. Decorate with "M&M's"® Chocolate Mini Baking Bits. Store in tightly covered container. *Makes about 84 cookies*

Orange Icing: In medium bowl combine 1 cup powdered sugar, 1 tablespoon water and 1 tablespoon pulp-free orange juice. Add additional water, 1 teaspoon at a time, if necessary to make icing spreadable.

Save Time

You can find specialty cookie cutters in the cake decorating section of craft stores. If you are in a hurry, cut the dough into circles or squares. Bake and frost as directed above; then use tubes of colorful frosting to print names, letters or numbers onto the cookie tops.

Handprints

1 package (20 ounces) refrigerated cookie dough, any flavor
All-purpose flour (optional)
Cookie glazes, frostings and assorted candies

1. Grease cookie sheets. Remove dough from wrapper according to package directions.

2. Cut dough into 4 equal sections. Reserve 1 section; refrigerate remaining 3 sections. Sprinkle reserved dough with flour to minimize sticking, if necessary. Roll dough on prepared cookie sheet to 5×7-inch rectangle.

3. Place hand, palm-side down, on dough. Carefully, cut around outline of hand with knife. Remove scraps. Separate dough fingers as much as possible using small spatula. Pat fingers outward to lengthen slightly. Repeat steps with remaining dough. Freeze dough handprints 15 minutes.

4. Preheat oven to 350°F.

5. Bake 7 to 13 minutes or until cookies are set and edges are golden brown. Cool completely on cookie sheets. Decorate as desired.

Makes 5 large handprint cookies

Make It Special

Get the kids involved by letting them use their own hands to make the handprints. Trace an outline of each child's hands on waxed paper. Label the outlines and use them to cut the cookie dough. The kids will enjoy seeing how their handprints bake into big cookies. For a quicker project, use one size hand for all the cookies. Then allow the kids to individually decorate their cookies.

Ice Cream Cone Cakes

1 package DUNCAN HINES® Moist Deluxe® Cake Mix (any flavor)
1 container DUNCAN HINES® Creamy Home-Style Chocolate Frosting
1 container DUNCAN HINES® Creamy Home-Style Vanilla Frosting
Chocolate sprinkles
Assorted decors
Jelly beans
2 maraschino cherries, for garnish

1. Preheat oven to 350°F. Grease and flour one 8-inch round cake pan and one 8-inch square pan.

2. Prepare cake following package directions for basic recipe. Pour about 2 cups batter into round pan. Pour about 3 cups batter into square pan. Bake at 350°F for 30 to 35 minutes or until toothpick inserted in center comes out clean. Cool following package directions.

3. To assemble, cut cooled cake and arrange as shown. Frost "cone" with Chocolate frosting, reserving ½ cup. Place writing tip in pastry bag. Fill with remaining ½ cup Chocolate frosting. Pipe waffle pattern onto "cones." Decorate with chocolate sprinkles. Spread Vanilla frosting on "ice cream." Decorate with assorted decors and jelly beans. Top each with maraschino cherry. *Makes 12 to 16 servings*

Tip: Use tip of knife to draw lines in frosting for waffle pattern as guide for piping chocolate frosting.

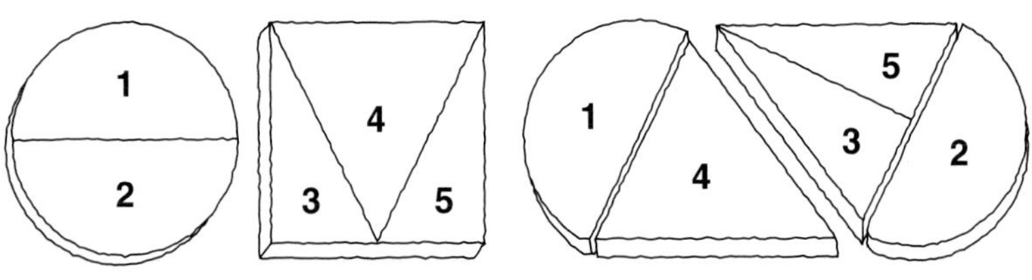

Chocolate X and O Cookies

⅔ **cup butter or margarine, softened**
1 cup sugar
2 teaspoons vanilla extract
2 eggs
2 tablespoons light corn syrup
2½ cups all-purpose flour
½ cup HERSHEY'S® Cocoa
½ teaspoon baking soda
¼ teaspoon salt
Decorating icing

1. Beat butter, sugar and vanilla in large bowl on medium speed of electric mixer until fluffy. Add eggs; beat well. Beat in corn syrup.

2. Combine flour, cocoa, baking soda and salt; gradually add to butter mixture, beating until well blended. Cover; refrigerate until dough is firm enough to handle.

3. Heat oven to 350°F. Shape dough into X and O shapes. Place on ungreased cookie sheet.

4. Bake 5 minutes or until set. Remove from cookie sheet to wire rack. Cool completely. Decorate as desired with icing.

Makes about 60 cookies

Preparation Hint

To shape X's: Shape rounded teaspoons of dough into 3-inch logs. Place 1 log on cookie sheet; press lightly in center. Place another 3-inch log on top of first one, forming X shape. To shape O's: Shape rounded teaspoon dough into 5-inch log. Connect ends, pressing lightly, forming O shape. Repeat for remaining O's.

Stripes

5½ cups cake batter,* divided
1 (10-inch) round cake board, covered, or large platter
1 container (about 16 ounces) white frosting
3 chocolate sandwich cookies
1 individual chocolate-covered cake roll
Pretzel sticks
Assorted candies and red licorice string
Chocolate sprinkles

**One prepared 18¼-ounce package of cake mix.*

1. Preheat oven to 350°F. Grease and flour 9-inch round cake pan and 8 standard (2½-inch) muffin cups.

2. Pour 3½ cups cake batter into cake pan; pour remaining cake batter into muffin cups (¼ cup batter per muffin cup). Bake cake in pan 35 to 45 minutes and cupcakes about 20 minutes or until toothpick inserted into centers comes out clean. Cool 15 minutes in pans. Loosen edges; invert onto wire racks and cool completely.

3. Trim tops and sides of round cake and 2 cupcakes. (Reserve remaining cupcakes for another use.) Place cake on prepared cake board. Position 2 cupcakes next to cake to form ears.

4. Tint frosting orange. Frost entire cake and cupcakes with orange frosting.

5. Carefully open 2 sandwich cookies to expose white filling. Place opened cookies on tiger's ears. Cut 2 thin slices from cake roll; place on tiger's face for eyes.

6. Add pretzel whiskers, cookie nose, candy mouth and chocolate sprinkle stripes as shown in photo. *Makes 12 to 14 servings*

Snowy Owl Cupcakes

1 package (about 18 ounces) white cake mix, plus ingredients to prepare mix
1 container (16 ounces) vanilla frosting
2½ cups sweetened, shredded coconut
48 round gummy candies
24 miniature (¾-inch) chocolate-covered mint candies, chocolate-covered raisins or black jelly beans
1 tube (0.6 ounce) black decorating gel

1. Line 24 standard (2½-inch) muffin cups with paper baking cups or spray with nonstick cooking spray.

2. Prepare cake mix and bake in muffin cups according to package directions. Cool in pans on wire racks 15 minutes. Remove to wire racks; cool completely.

3. Frost cupcakes with vanilla frosting. Sprinkle coconut over each cupcake, covering completely. Place 2 gummy candies on each cupcake for eyes. Add miniature chocolate-covered mint candy for beak. Use decorating gel to dot eyes. *Makes 24 cupcakes*

Make It Special

Novelty candles and candle holders are a quick and easy way to add fun, decorative flair to all kinds of cakes and cupcakes.

Yummy De-Lites

Serve up scrumptious treats made with healthful fruits, dried fruits and nuts, and a lot less fat, salt and sugar. Kids love them, and you can feel good knowing you're giving them the sweets they adore, but with more—goodness, that is.

Gingerbread Squares

3 tablespoons margarine, softened
2 tablespoons packed light brown sugar
¼ cup molasses
1 egg white
1¼ cups all-purpose flour
½ teaspoon baking soda
½ teaspoon ground ginger
½ teaspoon ground cinnamon
¼ teaspoon salt
1 cup sweetened applesauce
Decorations: tube frostings, colored sugars, red cinnamon candies or other small candies (optional)

1. Preheat oven to 350°F. Spray 8-inch square baking pan with nonstick cooking spray; set aside.

2. Beat margarine and sugar in medium bowl until well blended. Beat in molasses and egg white.

3. Combine dry ingredients in small bowl; mix well. Add to margarine mixture alternately with applesauce, mixing well after each addition. Transfer batter to prepared pan.

4. Bake 25 to 30 minutes or until toothpick inserted into center comes out clean. Cool completely on wire rack. Cut into 16 squares. Frost and decorate, if desired. *Makes 16 squares*

Crispy Rice Squares

- **3 tablespoons Dried Plum Purée (recipe follows) or prepared dried plum butter**
- **1 tablespoon butter or margarine**
- **1 package (10 ounces) marshmallows**
- **6 cups crisp rice cereal**
- **Colored nonpareils**

Coat 13×9-inch baking pan with vegetable cooking spray. Heat Dried Plum Purée and butter in Dutch oven or large saucepan over low heat, stirring until butter is melted. Add marshmallows; stir until completely melted. Remove from heat. Stir in cereal until well coated. Spray back of wooden spoon with vegetable cooking spray and pat mixture evenly into prepared pan. Sprinkle with nonpareils. Cool until set. Cut into squares. *Makes 24 squares*

Dried Plum Purée: Combine 1⅓ cups (8 ounces) pitted dried plums and ¼ cup plus 2 tablespoons hot water in container of food processor or blender. Pulse on and off until dried plums are finely chopped and smooth. Store leftovers in a covered container in the refrigerator for up to two months. Makes 1 cup.

Favorite recipe from **California Dried Plum Board**

Make It Special

To make Crispy Rice Squares even more festive, cut out shapes with cookie cutters. Double the recipe to make enough cut-outs for the whole class. Use the extra pieces to feed the kids, big and little, at home.

Cinnamon Apple Chips

2 cups unsweetened apple juice
1 cinnamon stick
2 Washington Red Delicious apples

1. In large skillet or saucepan, combine apple juice and cinnamon stick; bring to a low boil while preparing apples.

2. With paring knife, slice off ½ inch from tops and bottoms of apples and discard (or eat). Stand apples on either cut end; cut crosswise into ⅛-inch-thick slices, rotating apple as necessary to cut even slices.

3. Drop slices into boiling juice; cook 4 to 5 minutes or until slices appear translucent and lightly golden. Meanwhile, preheat oven to 250°F.

4. With slotted spatula, remove apple slices from juice and pat dry. Arrange slices on wire racks, making sure none overlap. Place racks on middle shelf in oven; bake 30 to 40 minutes until slices are lightly browned and almost dry to the touch. Let chips cool on racks completely before storing in airtight container.

Makes about 40 chips

Tip: There is no need to core apples. Boiling in juice several minutes softens core and removes seeds.

Favorite recipe from **Washington Apple Commission**

Make It Special

Many foods in this book also make great packed-lunch treats, after-school snacks and party surprises. Bake some delicious new treats for your family that are sure to command a repeat performance!

Strawberry Oat Mini Muffins

1 cup all-purpose flour
¾ cup uncooked oat bran cereal
2½ teaspoons baking powder
½ teaspoon baking soda
⅛ teaspoon salt
¾ cup buttermilk
⅓ cup frozen apple juice concentrate, thawed
⅓ cup unsweetened applesauce
½ teaspoon vanilla
¾ cup diced strawberries
¼ cup chopped pecans (optional)

1. Preheat oven to 400°F. Spray 24 mini (1¾-inch) muffin cups with nonstick cooking spray.

2. Combine flour, oat bran, baking powder, baking soda and salt in medium bowl. Whisk together buttermilk, apple juice concentrate, applesauce and vanilla in small bowl.

3. Stir buttermilk mixture into flour mixture until dry ingredients are almost moistened. Fold strawberries and pecans, if desired, into batter just until dry ingredients are moistened. *Do not overmix.*

4. Spoon batter into muffin cups. Bake 17 to 18 minutes or until lightly browned and toothpick inserted into centers comes out clean. Cool in pan on wire rack 5 minutes. Remove muffins to rack. Serve warm or cool completely. *Makes 24 muffins*

Strawberry Oat Mini Muffins

Snacking Surprise Muffins

1½ cups all-purpose flour
½ cup sugar
1 cup fresh or frozen blueberries
2½ teaspoons baking powder
1 teaspoon ground cinnamon
¼ teaspoon salt
1 egg, beaten
⅔ cup buttermilk
¼ cup margarine or butter, melted
3 tablespoons peach preserves

Topping
1 tablespoon sugar
¼ teaspoon ground cinnamon

1. Preheat oven to 400°F. Line 12 standard (2½-inch) muffin cups with paper baking cups; set aside.

2. Combine flour, ½ cup sugar, blueberries, baking powder, 1 teaspoon cinnamon and salt in medium bowl. Combine egg, buttermilk and margarine in small bowl. Add to flour mixture; mix just until moistened.

3. Spoon about 1 tablespoon batter into each muffin cup. Drop a scant teaspoonful of preserves into center of batter in each cup; top with remaining batter.

4. Combine 1 tablespoon sugar and ¼ teaspoon cinnamon in small bowl; sprinkle evenly over tops of batter.

5. Bake 18 to 20 minutes or until lightly browned. Remove muffins to wire rack to cool completely. *Makes 12 muffins*

Peach Gingerbread Muffins

2 cups all-purpose flour
2 teaspoons baking powder
1 teaspoon ground ginger
½ teaspoon salt
½ teaspoon ground cinnamon
¼ teaspoon ground cloves
½ cup sugar
½ cup MOTT'S® Chunky Apple Sauce
¼ cup MOTT'S® Apple Juice
¼ cup GRANDMA'S® Molasses
1 egg
2 tablespoons vegetable oil
1 (16-ounce) can peaches in juice, drained and chopped

1. Preheat oven to 400°F. Line 12 (2½-inch) muffin cups with paper liners or spray with nonstick cooking spray.

2. In large bowl, combine flour, baking powder, ginger, salt and spices.

3. In small bowl, combine sugar, apple sauce, apple juice, molasses, egg and oil.

4. Stir apple sauce mixture into flour mixture just until moistened. Fold in peaches.

5. Spoon batter evenly into prepared muffin cups.

6. Bake 20 minutes or until toothpick inserted in centers comes out clean. Immediately remove from pan; cool on wire rack 10 minutes. Serve warm or cool completely. *Makes 12 muffins*

Peach Gingerbread Muffins

Honey Carrot Snacking Cake

- **½ cup butter or margarine, softened**
- **1 cup honey**
- **2 eggs**
- **2 cups finely grated carrots**
- **½ cup golden raisins**
- **⅓ cup chopped nuts (optional)**
- **¼ cup orange juice**
- **2 teaspoons vanilla**
- **1 cup all-purpose flour**
- **1 cup whole wheat flour**
- **2 teaspoons baking powder**
- **1½ teaspoons ground cinnamon**
- **1 teaspoon baking soda**
- **½ teaspoon salt**
- **½ teaspoon ground ginger**
- **¼ teaspoon ground nutmeg**

Cream butter in large bowl. Gradually beat in honey until light and fluffy. Add eggs, one at a time, beating well after each addition. Combine carrots, raisins, nuts, if desired, orange juice and vanilla in medium bowl. Combine remaining dry ingredients in separate large bowl. Add dry ingredients to creamed mixture alternately with carrot mixture, beginning and ending with dry ingredients. Pour batter into greased 13×9×2-inch pan. Bake at 350°F 35 to 45 minutes or until wooden pick inserted near center comes out clean.

Makes 24 servings

Favorite recipe from **National Honey Board**

Honey Carrot Snacking Cake

Hikers' Bar Cookies

- **¾ cup all-purpose flour**
- **½ cup packed brown sugar**
- **½ cup uncooked quick oats**
- **¼ cup toasted wheat germ**
- **¼ cup unsweetened applesauce**
- **¼ cup margarine or butter, softened**
- **⅛ teaspoon salt**
- **½ cup egg substitute**
- **¼ cup raisins**
- **¼ cup dried cranberries**
- **¼ cup sunflower kernels**
- **1 tablespoon grated orange peel**
- **1 teaspoon ground cinnamon**

1. Preheat oven to 350°F. Lightly coat 13×9-inch baking pan with nonstick cooking spray; set aside.

2. Beat flour, sugar, oats, wheat germ, applesauce, margarine and salt in large bowl with electric mixer at medium speed until well blended. Stir in egg substitute, raisins, cranberries, sunflower kernels, orange peel and cinnamon. Spread into pan.

3. Bake 15 minutes or until firm to touch. Cool completely in pan. Cut into 24 squares.

Makes 24 servings

Blueberry Orange Muffins

1¾ cups all-purpose flour
⅓ cup sugar
2½ teaspoons baking powder
½ teaspoon baking soda
½ teaspoon salt
½ teaspoon ground cinnamon
¾ cup fat-free (skim) milk
1 egg, lightly beaten
¼ cup (½ stick) butter, melted and slightly cooled
3 tablespoons orange juice concentrate, thawed
1 teaspoon vanilla
¾ cup fresh or frozen blueberries, thawed

1. Preheat oven to 400°F. Grease or line 12 standard (2½-inch) muffin cups with paper baking cups.

2. Combine flour, sugar, baking powder, baking soda, salt and cinnamon in large bowl. Set aside.

3. Beat milk, egg, butter, orange juice concentrate and vanilla in medium bowl on medium speed of electric mixer until well combined.

4. Add milk mixture to dry ingredients. Mix lightly until dry ingredients are barely moistened (mixture will be lumpy). Add blueberries. Stir gently just until berries are evenly distributed.

5. Fill muffin cups ¾ full. Bake 20 to 25 minutes (25 to 30 minutes if using frozen berries) or until toothpick inserted into centers comes out clean. Let cool 5 minutes in pan; remove from pan to wire rack. Serve warm.

Makes 12 muffins

Rollers & Wraps

For a creative alternative to sweet snacks, fill the crowd up with miniature sandwiches—rolled or wrapped—for neat, fun-to-eat snacks.

Sweet Treat Tortillas

8 (7- to 8-inch) flour tortillas
1 package (8 ounces) Neufchâtel cheese, softened
½ cup strawberry or other flavor fruit spread
2 medium bananas, peeled and chopped

1. Spread each tortilla with 1 ounce Neufchâtel cheese and 1 tablespoon fruit spread; top with ¼ of the chopped bananas.

2. Roll up tortillas; wrap individually in plastic wrap or place in covered plastic container. Refrigerate until ready to serve.

3. To serve, cut each roll crosswise into thirds. Place in insulated bags with frozen ice packs to carry to school. *Makes 24 rolls*

More Sweet Treats: Substitute your favorite chopped fruit for bananas.

Cinnamon-Spice Treats: Omit fruit spread and bananas. Mix small amounts of sugar, ground cinnamon and nutmeg to taste into Neufchâtel cheese; spread evenly onto tortillas. Top with chopped fruit or raisins, if desired; roll up. Cut crosswise into thirds.

Sweet Treat Tortillas

Pizza Snack Cups

1 can (12 ounces) refrigerated biscuits (10 biscuits)
½ pound ground beef
1 jar (14 ounces) RAGÚ® Pizza Quick® Sauce
½ cup shredded mozzarella cheese (about 2 ounces)

1. Preheat oven to 375°F. In muffin pan, evenly press each biscuit in bottom and up side of each cup; chill until ready to fill.

2. In 10-inch skillet, brown ground beef over medium-high heat; drain. Stir in Ragú Pizza Quick Sauce and heat through. Evenly spoon beef mixture into prepared muffin cups. Bake 15 minutes. Sprinkle with cheese and bake an additional 5 minutes or until cheese is melted and biscuits are golden. Let stand 5 minutes. Gently remove pizza cups from muffin pan and serve. *Makes 10 pizza cups*

Note: Carry pizza cups to school in muffin pans or place cups in covered disposable aluminum pans. Pack in insulated bags to keep warm, or reheat in pans at school.

Pizza Snack Cups

Rock 'n' Rollers

8 (6- to 7-inch) flour tortillas
1 package (8 ounces) Neufchâtel cheese, softened
⅔ cup peach preserves
2 cups (8 ounces) shredded Cheddar cheese
1 cup packed stemmed fresh spinach leaves
6 ounces thinly sliced regular or smoked turkey breast

1. Spread each tortilla evenly with 1 ounce Neufchâtel cheese; cover with thin layer of preserves. Sprinkle with Cheddar cheese.

2. Arrange spinach leaves and turkey over Cheddar cheese. Roll up tortillas; trim ends. Place rollers in covered plastic container. Refrigerate until ready to serve.

3. Pack containers in insulated bags with frozen ice packs. To serve, cut each roller crosswise in half or diagonally into 1-inch pieces.

Makes 16 to 24 roll-up slices

Sassy Salsa Rollers: Substitute salsa for peach preserves and shredded iceberg lettuce for spinach leaves.

Ham 'n' Apple Rollers: Omit peach preserves and spinach leaves. Substitute lean ham slices for turkey. Spread tortillas with Neufchâtel cheese as directed; sprinkle with Cheddar cheese. Top each tortilla with about 2 tablespoons finely chopped apple and 2 ham slices; roll up. Continue as directed.

Play It Safe

Keep hot food hot and cold food cold: 140°F or above for hot food, 40°F or below for cold food. To keep food cool, use an insulated bag with a frozen ice pack. Carry hot food in a thermos or insulated bag.

Rock 'n' Rollers

Stuffed Bundles

1 package (about 10 ounces) refrigerated pizza dough
2 ounces lean ham or turkey-ham, chopped
½ cup (2 ounces) shredded sharp Cheddar cheese

1. Preheat oven to 425°F. Spray 12 standard (2½-inch) muffin cups with nonstick cooking spray.

2. Unroll dough on flat surface; cut into 12 pieces (about 4×3-inch rectangles). Divide ham and cheese between dough rectangles. Bring corners of dough together, pinching to seal. Place smooth side up in prepared muffin cups.

3. Bake 10 to 12 minutes or until golden. Cool slightly. Pack in covered disposable aluminum pans. Place in insulated bags to keep warm, or reheat and serve. *Makes 12 bundles*

Kids' Quesadillas

8 slices American cheese
8 (10-inch) flour tortillas
½ pound thinly sliced deli turkey
6 tablespoons *French's*® Sweet & Tangy Honey Mustard
2 tablespoons melted butter
¼ teaspoon paprika

1. To prepare 1 quesadilla, arrange 2 slices of cheese on 1 tortilla. Top with one fourth of the turkey. Spread with *1½ tablespoons* mustard, then top with another tortilla. Prepare 3 more quesadillas with remaining ingredients.

2. Combine butter and paprika. Brush one side of tortilla with butter mixture. Preheat 12-inch nonstick skillet over medium-high heat. Arrange tortilla butter side down and cook 2 minutes. Brush tortilla with butter mixture and turn over. Cook 1½ minutes or until golden brown. Repeat with remaining three quesadillas. Slice into wedges before serving. *Makes 4 servings*

Note: Carry quesadillas to school in covered disposable aluminum pans. Pack in insulated bags to keep warm.

Dizzy Dogs

1 to 2 packages refrigerated breadstick dough (8 breadsticks)
2 packages (16 ounces each) hot dogs (16 hot dogs)
2 egg whites
Sesame and/or poppy seeds
Mustard, ketchup and barbecue sauce (optional)

1. Preheat oven to 375°F.

2. Using 1 breadstick for each, wrap hot dogs with dough in spiral pattern. Brush breadstick dough with egg white and sprinkle with sesame and/or poppy seeds. Place on ungreased baking sheet.

3. Bake 12 to 15 minutes or until light golden brown. Cool slightly. Place in covered disposable aluminum pans. Carry to school in insulated bags. Serve immediately or reheat and serve with condiments for dipping, if desired. *Makes 16 hot dogs*

Taco Cups

1 pound lean ground beef, turkey or pork
1 package (1 ounce) LAWRY'S® Taco Spices & Seasonings
1¼ cups water
¼ cup salsa
2 packages (8 ounces each) refrigerator biscuits
½ cup (2 ounces) shredded cheddar cheese

In medium skillet, brown ground beef until crumbly; drain fat. Stir in Taco Spices & Seasonings and water. Bring to a boil; reduce heat to low and cook, uncovered, 10 minutes. Stir in salsa. Separate biscuits and press each biscuit into an ungreased muffin cup. Spoon equal amounts of meat mixture into each muffin cup; sprinkle each with cheese. Bake, uncovered, in 350°F oven for 12 minutes.

Makes about 16 taco cups

Note: Cool cups slightly in pans. Cover and pack muffin pans in insulated bags to carry to school. Serve immediately or reheat in pans.

Chicken Tortilla Roll-Ups

1 package (8 ounces) cream cheese, softened
¼ cup mayonnaise
2 tablespoons Dijon mustard (optional)
½ teaspoon black pepper
6 (10- to 12-inch) flour tortillas
2 cups finely chopped cooked chicken
1½ cups shredded or finely chopped carrots
1½ cups finely chopped green bell pepper

1. Combine cream cheese, mayonnaise, mustard, if desired, and black pepper in small bowl; stir until well blended.

2. Spread cream cheese mixture evenly onto each tortilla, leaving ½-inch border. Divide chicken, if desired, carrot and bell pepper evenly over cream cheese, leaving 1½-inch border on cream cheese mixture at one end of each tortilla.

3. Roll up each tortilla jelly-roll fashion. Refrigerate until ready to serve. Cut each roll into 1½-inch-thick slices.

Makes 24 to 30 roll-up slices

Make It Special

Wrap the rolls in plastic wrap and refrigerate them for several hours for easier slicing and a better blend of flavors.

Cold Pizza Rolls

2 tablespoons cornmeal, divided
1 package (about 14 ounces) refrigerated pizza dough
6 ounces thinly sliced Canadian bacon
⅓ cup crushed pineapple, well drained
⅓ cup pizza sauce
3 pieces (1 ounce each) string cheese

1. Preheat oven to 400°F. Spray large baking sheet with nonstick cooking spray. Lightly sprinkle with 1 tablespoon cornmeal.

2. Roll pizza dough into 16½×11-inch rectangle on lightly floured surface. Lightly sprinkle with remaining 1 tablespoon cornmeal. Cut into 6 squares. Top each square with bacon, pineapple and pizza sauce.

3. Cut each piece of string cheese in half. Place 1 piece of cheese on each square. Bring up 2 opposite sides of each square together and seal. Place rolls, seam side down, on prepared baking sheet. Crimp ends of each roll to seal.

4. Bake 15 to 17 minutes or until golden. Cool completely on wire rack. Wrap each in plastic wrap. Refrigerate 2 hours or overnight.

Makes 6 servings (1 roll each)

Prep Time: 10 minutes • Bake Time: 17 minutes

Tasty Teaching Time

Sandwiches and snacks are a lot more likely to be eaten if they are served in smaller sizes. Small portions not only prevent the wasting of food, but encourage students to taste unfamiliar foods that they might not otherwise try.

Rainbow Spirals

4 (10-inch) flour tortillas (assorted flavors and colors)
4 tablespoons *French's®* Mustard (any flavor)
½ pound (about 8 slices) thinly sliced deli roast beef, bologna or turkey
8 slices American, provolone or Muenster cheese
Fancy Party Toothpicks

1. Spread each tortilla with *1 tablespoon* mustard. Layer with meat and cheeses, dividing evenly.

2. Roll up jelly-roll style; secure with toothpicks and cut into thirds. Arrange on platter. *Makes 12 roll-up slices*

Prep Time: 10 minutes

Note: For classroom treats, eliminate the toothpicks. Wrap each roll securely in plastic wrap. Refrigerate before cutting to serve.

Monster Finger Sandwiches

2 cans (11 ounces) refrigerated breadstick dough (12 breadsticks)
Mustard
24 slices deli ham, cut into ½-inch strips
8 slices Monterey Jack cheese, cut into ½-inch strips
2 egg yolks, lightly beaten
Assorted food colorings

1. Preheat oven to 350°F. Place 6 breadsticks on ungreased baking sheets. Spread with mustard as desired. Divide ham strips evenly among breadsticks, placing over mustard. Repeat with cheese. Top with remaining 6 breadsticks. Gently stretch top dough over filling; press dough together to seal.

2. Score knuckle and nail lines into each sandwich using sharp knife. Do not cut completely through dough. Tint egg yolk with food coloring as desired. Paint nail with egg yolk mixture.

3. Bake on lower oven rack 12 to 13 minutes or just until golden. Let cool slightly. Serve warm or cool completely. *Makes 12 servings*

Rainbow Spirals

Peanut Butter-Apple Wraps

¾ cup creamy peanut butter
4 (7-inch) whole wheat flour or spinach tortillas or 8-grain lavash
¾ cup finely chopped apple
⅓ cup shredded carrot
⅓ cup low-fat granola without raisins
1 tablespoon toasted wheat germ

Spread peanut butter onto 1 side of each tortilla. Sprinkle each tortilla with one fourth of apple, carrot, granola and wheat germ evenly over each tortilla. Roll up tightly; cut in half. Serve immediately or refrigerate until ready to serve. *Makes 8 servings*

Prep Time: 5 minutes • Chill Time: 2 hours

Tasty Teaching Time

Food wrapped in edible bundles always tastes twice as nice. Flour tortilla wraps like these Peanut Butter-Apple Wraps are one child-friendly way to contribute toward the recommended servings of fruits and vegetables for a day.

Last-Minute Treats

Oh my! You promised to bring classroom treats and just ran out of time. This chapter saves the day with tasty, easy-to-prepare treats.

Chocolate Cherry Cupcakes

1 package (about 18 ounces) devil's food cake mix
1⅓ cups water
3 eggs
½ cup sour cream
⅓ cup oil
1 cup dried cherries
1 container (16 ounces) buttercream frosting, divided
25 drops green food coloring
11 maraschino cherries, stemmed and halved

1. Preheat oven to 350°F. Line 22 standard (2½-inch) muffin cups with paper baking cups.

2. Beat cake mix, water, eggs, sour cream and oil in large bowl 30 seconds at low speed of electric mixer or until just blended. Beat on medium speed 2 minutes or until smooth. Fold in dried cherries.

3. Fill muffin cups ¾ full with batter. Bake 20 to 24 minutes or until toothpick inserted into centers comes out clean. Cool in pan on wire rack 10 minutes. Remove from pan to wire rack; cool completely.

4. Place ¼ cup frosting in small bowl with food coloring; stir to combine. Set aside.

5. Frost cupcakes with remaining white frosting. Place 1 cherry half, cut side down, on each cupcake. Place green frosting in piping bag fitted with writing tip. Pipe a stem and leaf onto each cupcake.

Makes 22 cupcakes

Sugar-and-Spice Twists

1 tablespoon sugar
¼ teaspoon ground cinnamon
1 package (6-count) refrigerated breadstick dough

1. Preheat oven to 350°F. Spray baking sheet with nonstick cooking spray; set aside.

2. Combine sugar and cinnamon in shallow dish or plate; set aside.

3. Divide breadstick dough into 6 pieces. Roll each piece into 12-inch rope. Roll in sugar-cinnamon mixture. Twist into pretzel shape. Place on prepared baking sheet. Bake 15 to 18 minutes or until lightly browned. Remove from baking sheet. Cool 5 minutes. Serve warm.

Makes 6 servings

Hint: Use colored sugar sprinkles in place of the sugar in this recipe for a fun 'twist' of color that's perfect for holidays, birthdays or simple everyday celebrations.

Quick & Easy Pumpkin Cupcakes

1 package (18.25 ounces) spice cake mix
1 can (15 ounces) LIBBY'S® 100% Pure Pumpkin
3 large eggs
⅓ cup vegetable oil
⅓ cup water
1 container (16 ounces) prepared cream cheese or vanilla frosting
Assorted sprinkles

PREHEAT oven to 350°F. Paper-line or grease 24 muffin cups.

BLEND cake mix, pumpkin, eggs, vegetable oil and water in large mixer bowl until moistened. Beat on medium speed for 2 minutes. Pour batter into prepared muffin cups, filling ¾ full.

BAKE for 18 to 23 minutes or until wooden pick inserted in centers comes out clean. Cool in pan on wire rack for 10 minutes; remove to wire racks to cool completely. Spread cupcakes with frosting. Decorate as desired.

Makes 24 cupcakes

Sugar-and-Spice Twists

Conversation Heart Cereal Treats

20 large marshmallows
2 tablespoons margarine or butter
3 cups frosted oat cereal with marshmallow bits
16 large conversation hearts

1. Line 8- or 9-inch square pan with aluminum foil, leaving 2-inch overhang on 2 sides. Generously grease or spray with nonstick cooking spray.

2. Melt marshmallows and margarine in medium saucepan over medium heat 3 minutes or until melted and smooth, stirring constantly. Remove from heat.

3. Add cereal; stir until completely coated. Spread in prepared pan; press evenly onto bottom using greased rubber spatula. Press heart candies into top of treats while still warm, evenly spacing to allow 1 heart per bar. Let cool 10 minutes. Using foil, remove treats from pan. Cut into 16 bars. *Makes 16 bars*

Prep and Cook Time: 18 minutes

Conversation Heart Cereal Treats

Hershey®'s Easy Chocolate Cracker Snacks

1⅔ cups (10-ounce package) HERSHEY®'S Mint Chocolate Chips*
2 cups (12-ounce package) HERSHEY®'S Semi-Sweet Chocolate Chips
2 tablespoons shortening (do not use butter, margarine, spread or oil)
60 to 70 round buttery crackers (about one-half 1-pound box)

**2 cups (11.5-ounce package) HERSHEY®'S Milk Chocolate Chips and ¼ teaspoon pure peppermint extract can be substituted for mint chocolate chips.*

1. Line several trays or cookie sheets with waxed paper.

2. Place mint chocolate chips, chocolate chips and shortening in large microwave-safe bowl. Microwave at HIGH (100%) 1 minute; stir. Continue heating 30 seconds at a time, stirring after each heating, until chips are melted and mixture is smooth when stirred.

3. Drop crackers into chocolate mixture one at a time. Using tongs, push cracker into chocolate so that it is covered completely. (If chocolate begins to thicken, reheat 10 to 20 seconds in microwave.) Remove from chocolate, tapping lightly on edge of bowl to remove excess chocolate. Place on prepared tray. Refrigerate until chocolate hardens, about 20 minutes. For best results, store tightly covered in refrigerator. *Makes about 66 snacks*

Peanut Butter and Milk Chocolate: Use 1⅔ cups (10-ounce package) REESE'S® Peanut Butter Chips, 2 cups (11.5-ounce package) HERSHEY®'S Milk Chocolate Chips and 2 tablespoons shortening. Proceed as above.

Chocolate Raspberry: Use 1⅔ cups (10-ounce package) HERSHEY®'S Raspberry Chips, 2 cups (11.5-ounce package) HERSHEY®'S Milk Chocolate Chips and 2 tablespoons shortening. Proceed as above.

White Chip and Toffee: Melt 1⅔ cups (10-ounce package) HERSHEY®'S Premier White Chips and 1 tablespoon shortening. Dip crackers; before coating hardens, sprinkle with SKOR® English Toffee Bits or HEATH® BITS 'O BRICKLE® Almond Toffee Bits.

Hershey's® Easy Chocolate Cracker Snacks

Brownie Gems

- 1 package DUNCAN HINES® Chocolate Lover's® Double Fudge Brownie Mix
- 2 eggs
- 2 tablespoons water
- ⅓ cup vegetable oil
- 28 miniature peanut butter cup or chocolate kiss candies
- 1 container of your favorite Duncan Hines frosting

1. Preheat oven to 350°F. Spray (1¾-inch) mini-muffin pans with vegetable cooking spray or line with foil baking cups.

2. Combine brownie mix, fudge packet from mix, eggs, water and oil in large bowl. Stir with spoon until well blended, about 50 strokes. Drop 1 heaping teaspoonful of batter into each muffin cup; top with candy. Cover candy with more batter. Bake at 350°F for 15 to 17 minutes.

3. Cool 5 minutes. Carefully loosen brownies from pan. Remove to wire racks to cool completely. Frost and decorate as desired.

Makes 28 brownie gems

Number One Cake

- 1 (13×9-inch) cake
- 1 (19×13-inch) cake board, cut in half crosswise and covered
- 1½ cups prepared white frosting
- Yellow food coloring
- Assorted colored candies

1. Trim top and sides of cake. Draw a number 1 pattern on 13×9-inch piece of waxed paper. Cut pattern out and place on cake. Cut out cake around the pattern; place on prepared cake board. Reserve extra cake for another use, if desired.

2. Tint frosting yellow; frost cake. Decorate with assorted candies as desired.

Makes 16 servings

Crispy Cocoa Bars

¼ cup (½ stick) margarine
¼ cup HERSHEY®S Cocoa
5 cups miniature marshmallows
5 cups crisp rice cereal

1. Spray 13×9×2-inch pan with vegetable cooking spray.

2. Melt margarine in large saucepan over low heat; stir in cocoa and marshmallows. Cook over low heat, stirring constantly, until marshmallows are melted and mixture is smooth and well blended. Continue cooking 1 minute, stirring constantly. Remove from heat.

3. Add cereal; stir until coated. Lightly spray spatula with vegetable cooking spray; press mixture into prepared pan. Cool completely. Cut into bars. *Makes 24 bars*

Contents

Cookie Sundae Cups

1 package (18 ounces) refrigerated chocolate chip cookie dough
6 cups ice cream, any flavor
1¼ cups ice cream topping, any flavor
Whipped cream
Colored sprinkles

1. Preheat oven to 350°F. Lightly grease 18 (2½-inch) muffin pan cups.

2. Remove dough from wrapper. Shape dough into 18 balls; press onto bottoms and up sides of prepared muffin cups.

3. Bake 14 to 18 minutes or until golden brown. Cool in muffin cups 10 minutes. Remove to wire rack; cool completely.

4. Place ⅓ cup ice cream in each cookie cup. Drizzle with ice cream topping. Top with whipped cream and colored sprinkles. *Makes 1½ dozen desserts*

Burger Bliss

Buns

1 package (18 ounces) refrigerated sugar cookie dough
½ cup creamy peanut butter
⅓ cup all-purpose flour
¼ cup packed light brown sugar
½ teaspoon vanilla
Beaten egg white and sesame seeds (optional)

Burgers

½ (18-ounce) package refrigerated sugar cookie dough
3 tablespoons unsweetened cocoa powder
2 tablespoons packed light brown sugar
½ teaspoon vanilla
Red, yellow and green decorating icings

1. Preheat oven to 350°F. Grease cookie sheets. For buns, remove dough from wrapper; place in large bowl. Let stand at room temperature 15 minutes. Add peanut butter, flour, brown sugar and vanilla to dough; beat until blended. Shape into 48 (1-inch) balls; place 2 inches apart on cookie sheets.

2. Bake 14 minutes or until browned. If desired, remove from oven after 10 minutes; brush with egg white and sprinkle with sesame seeds. Return to oven; bake 4 minutes. Cool on cookie sheets 2 to 3 minutes. Remove to wire racks; cool completely.

3. For burgers, remove half of dough from wrapper. (Reserve remaining dough for another use.) Beat dough, cocoa, brown sugar and vanilla in bowl until blended. Shape into 24 (1-inch) balls; place 2 inches apart on cookie sheets. Flatten cookies to ¼-inch thickness with a diameter slightly larger than buns.

4. Bake 12 minutes or until firm. Cool on cookie sheets 2 to 3 minutes. Remove to wire rack; cool completely.

5. To assemble, use icing to attach burgers to flat sides of 24 buns; pipe red, yellow and green icings on burgers. Top with remaining buns. *Makes 2 dozen sandwich cookies*

Cookie Fondue

Cookie Dippers

1 package (18 ounces) refrigerated oatmeal raisin cookie dough

1 cup powdered sugar

1 egg

Chocolate Sauce

½ cup semisweet chocolate chips

¼ cup heavy cream

White Chocolate Sauce

½ cup white chocolate chips

¼ cup heavy cream

Strawberry-Marshmallow Sauce

¼ cup strawberry syrup

¼ cup marshmallow creme

1. For dippers, preheat oven to 350°F. Grease cookie sheets. Remove dough from wrapper; place in large bowl. Let dough stand at room temperature about 15 minutes. Add powdered sugar and egg to dough; beat until well blended. Drop dough by teaspoonfuls onto prepared cookie sheets. Bake 8 minutes or until edges are lightly browned. Cool on cookie sheets 5 minutes. Remove to wire rack; cool completely.

2. For chocolate sauce, mix semisweet chocolate chips and cream in microwavable bowl. Heat on HIGH 20 seconds; stir. Heat on HIGH at additional 20-second intervals until melted and smooth; stir well after each interval. For white chocolate sauce, repeat with white chocolate chips and cream.

3. For strawberry-marshmallow sauce, mix strawberry syrup and marshmallow creme in small bowl; stir until smooth. Serve cookie dippers with sauces. *Makes 2½ dozen cookies*

Hint: Serve sauces in small bowls along with small bowls of chopped nuts, coconut and dried cranberries for double dipping.

Chocolate Truffle Cookies

1 package (18 ounces) refrigerated sugar cookie dough
⅓ cup unsweetened cocoa powder
1 tablespoon powdered sugar
½ teaspoon vanilla
1 package (12 ounces) milk chocolate-covered chewy chocolate caramel candies (¾-inch squares)
¾ cup semisweet chocolate chips
Colored sprinkles

1. Preheat oven to 325°F. Line cookie sheets with parchment paper. Remove dough from wrapper; place in large bowl. Let dough stand at room temperature about 15 minutes.

2. Add cocoa, powdered sugar and vanilla to dough; beat at medium speed of electric mixer until well blended.

3. Shape about 2 teaspoons dough into ball; wrap ball around 1 caramel candy. Repeat with remaining dough and candies. Place filled balls 2 inches apart on prepared cookie sheets. Bake 12 to 15 minutes or until set. Remove to wire rack; cool completely.

4. Place wire rack over waxed paper. Place chocolate chips in small microwavable bowl. Microwave on HIGH 1 to 1½ minutes. Stir after 1 minute and at 30-second intervals after first minute until chips are melted and smooth.

5. Spoon small amount of chocolate on top of each cookie; top with sprinkles. Let stand on wire rack until set. Store in refrigerator. *Makes about 3 dozen cookies*

Watermelon Slices

2 packages (18 ounces each) refrigerated sugar cookie dough, divided
½ cup all-purpose flour, divided
Green and red food colorings
Mini chocolate chips

1. Remove both sugar doughs from wrappers; place in separate medium bowls. Let stand at room temperature about 15 minutes. Add ¼ cup flour and green food coloring to dough in one bowl; beat at medium speed of electric mixer until well blended and evenly colored. Wrap in plastic wrap; refrigerate about 2 hours.

2. Add remaining ¼ cup flour and red food coloring to dough in remaining bowl; beat at medium speed of electric mixer until well blended and evenly colored. Shape into 9-inch-long log. Sprinkle with flour to minimize sticking, if necessary. Wrap in plastic wrap; refrigerate about 2 hours.

3. Remove green dough from refrigerator. Roll between sheets of waxed paper to 9×8-inch rectangle. Remove plastic wrap from red dough log; place in center of green rectangle.

4. Fold green edges up and around red dough log; press seam together. Roll gently to form smooth log. Wrap in plastic wrap. Freeze 30 minutes.

5. Preheat oven to 350°F. Remove waxed paper. Cut log into ⅜-inch-thick slices. Cut each slice in half. Place 2 inches apart on ungreased cookie sheets. Gently re-shape, if necessary. Press several mini chocolate chips into each slice for watermelon seeds. Bake 8 to 11 minutes or until set. Cool on cookie sheets 1 minute. Remove to wire racks; cool completely.

Makes about 5 dozen cookies

Congrats Grad

1 package (18 ounces) refrigerated sugar cookie dough
¼ cup *each* all-purpose flour and creamy peanut butter
1 cup mini chocolate chips
Granulated sugar
48 small gumdrops to match school colors
Cookie Glaze (recipe follows)
Food colorings to match school colors
12 graham cracker squares

1. Preheat oven to 350°F. Grease 12 (2½-inch) muffin cups. Remove dough from wrapper. Beat dough, flour and peanut butter in large bowl until well blended. Stir in chocolate chips. Shape dough into 12 balls; press onto bottoms and up sides of prepared muffin cups.

2. Bake 15 to 18 minutes or until browned; let cool in pan on wire rack 10 minutes. Remove from pan; cool completely.

3. Sprinkle sugar on waxed paper. For each tassel, slightly flatten 3 gumdrops. Place gumdrops, with ends overlapping slightly, on sugared surface. Sprinkle with additional sugar as needed. Roll flattened gumdrops into 3×1-inch piece with rolling pin, turning piece over often to coat with sugar. Trim and discard edges of gumdrop piece. Cut piece into 2½×¼-inch strips. Cut bottom part into several lengthwise strips to form fringe.

4. Prepare Cookie Glaze; tint desired color. Place cookies upside down on wire racks set over waxed paper. Spread glaze over cookies to cover. Spread glaze over graham crackers. Set cracker on top of each cookie. Place tassel on each cap; top with gumdrop. Let stand 40 minutes or until glaze is set.

Makes 1 dozen large cookies

Cookie Glaze: Combine 4 cups powdered sugar and 6 to 8 tablespoons milk, 1 tablespoon at a time, to make medium-thick pourable glaze.

Congrats Grad

Double Chocolate Sandwich Cookies

1 package (18 ounces) refrigerated sugar cookie dough
1 bar (3½ to 4 ounces) bittersweet chocolate, chopped
2 teaspoons butter
¾ cup milk chocolate chips

1. Preheat oven to 350°F. Remove dough from wrapper, keeping in log shape.

2. Cut dough into ¼-inch-thick slices. Arrange slices 2 inches apart on ungreased cookie sheets. Cut centers out of half the cookies using 1-inch round cookie cutter.

3. Bake 10 to 12 minutes or until edges are lightly browned. Let stand on cookie sheets 2 minutes. Remove to wire rack; cool completely.

4. Place bittersweet chocolate and butter in small heavy saucepan. Heat over low heat, stirring frequently, until chocolate is melted. Spread chocolate over flat sides of cookies without holes. Immediately top each with cutout cookie.

5. Place milk chocolate chips in resealable food storage bag; seal bag. Microwave on MEDIUM (50%) 1½ minutes. Turn bag over; microwave 1 to 1½ minutes or until melted. Knead bag until chocolate is smooth.

6. Cut tiny corner off bag; drizzle chocolate decoratively over sandwich cookies. Let stand until chocolate is set, about 30 minutes.

Makes 16 sandwich cookies

Hockey Sticks & Pucks

1 package (18 ounces) refrigerated sugar cookie dough
¾ cup all-purpose flour
24 miniature (¾-inch) chocolate-covered mint candies
Prepared icings

1. Grease cookie sheets. Remove dough from wrapper; place in large bowl. Let dough stand at room temperature 15 minutes.

2. Add flour to dough; knead until well blended. Divide dough into 24 pieces. Shape each piece into 6-inch-long rope. Place ropes on prepared cookie sheets; bend ropes about 1¾ inches from ends to form hockey stick shapes. Freeze 10 minutes.

3. Preheat oven to 350°F. Bake 8 to 10 minutes or until lightly browned. While cookies are still hot, place one mint on bottom part of each cookie for puck. Cool completely on cookie sheets.

4. Decorate with icings as desired.

Makes 2 dozen cookies

Nothin' But Net

1 package (18 ounces) refrigerated sugar cookie dough
1¼ cups all-purpose flour
2 tablespoons *each* powdered sugar and lemon juice
Orange, white and black decorating icings

1. Remove dough from wrapper; place in large bowl. Let dough stand at room temperature about 15 minutes.

2. Add flour, powdered sugar and lemon juice to dough; beat until well blended. Divide dough in half. Wrap each half in plastic wrap; refrigerate at least 2 hours. Meanwhile, make pattern out of clean, lightweight cardboard using diagram.

3. Preheat oven to 350°F. Grease cookie sheets. Roll 1 dough half to ¼-inch thickness on lightly floured surface. Place pattern, sprayed side down, on dough. Cut around pattern with sharp knife; remove pattern from dough. Place cutouts 2 inches apart on prepared cookie sheets. Repeat with remaining dough.

4. Bake 13 to 15 minutes or until edges are lightly browned. Remove to wire rack; cool completely.Decorate with icings as shown in photo. *Makes 1½ dozen cookies*

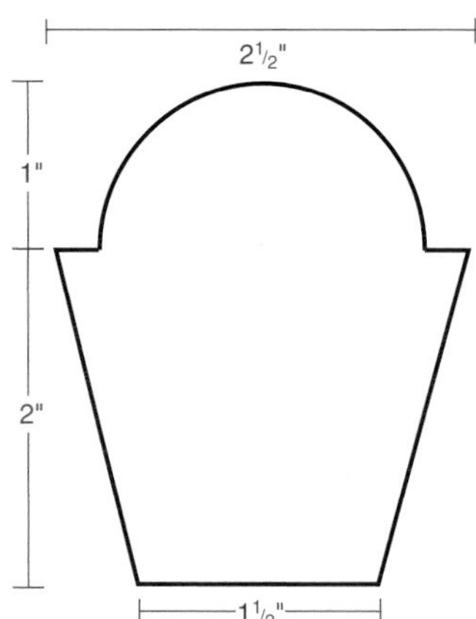

Nothin' But Net

Building Blocks

1 package (18 ounces) refrigerated cookie dough, any flavor
Powdered Sugar Glaze (recipe follows)
Assorted food colorings
Assorted round fruit-flavored gummy candies (about ¼ inch in diameter)

1. Preheat oven to 350°F. Grease 13×9-inch baking pan.

2. Remove dough from wrapper; place in large bowl. Let dough stand at room temperature about 15 minutes.

3. Press dough evenly onto bottom of prepared pan. Score dough lengthwise and crosswise into 32 equal rectangles (about 1½×2¼ inches each) with sharp knife. Freeze 10 minutes.

4. Bake 10 minutes; remove from oven. Re-score partially baked cookies. Return pan to oven; bake 4 to 5 minutes or until edges are lightly browned and center is set. Cut through score marks to separate cookies. Cool in pan 10 minutes. Remove to wire rack; cool completely.

5. Prepare Powdered Sugar Glaze; divide into 3 or 4 bowls. Tint glaze with food colorings as desired.

6. Place wire rack over waxed paper. Spread glaze over tops and sides of cookies. Let stand about 5 minutes; place 6 gummy candies on each cookie. Let stand about 40 minutes or until completely set. *Makes about 2½ dozen cookies*

Powdered Sugar Glaze: Combine 2 cups powdered sugar and 6 tablespoons heavy cream in medium bowl; whisk until smooth. Add 1 to 2 tablespoons cream, 1 tablespoon at a time, to make medium-thick pourable glaze.

Snickerdoodle Batter-Ups

1 package (18 ounces) refrigerated sugar cookie dough
1 teaspoon vanilla
¼ cup sugar
¼ teaspoon ground cinnamon
Chocolate and red decorating icings

1. Remove dough from wrapper; place in medium bowl. Let dough stand at room temperature about 15 minutes.

2. Add vanilla to dough; beat until well blended. Divide dough in half. Wrap each half in plastic wrap; refrigerate 1 hour.

3. Preheat oven to 350°F. For baseballs, roll 1 dough half to ¼-inch thickness on well-floured surface using well-floured rolling pin. Cut dough into circles using 2½-inch round cookie cutter. Reroll dough and scraps, if necessary, to make 12 circles.

4. Place cutouts on ungreased cookie sheets. Mix sugar and cinnamon in bowl; sprinkle over cutouts. Bake 8 to 10 minutes or until firm and edges are lightly browned. Cool on cookie sheets 3 minutes. Remove to wire rack; cool completely.

5. For bats, make pattern for bat out of clean, lightweight cardboard using diagram. (Or use 4-inch baseball bat-shaped cookie cutter.) Roll remaining dough half to ¼-inch thickness on well-floured surface using well-floured rolling pin. Place pattern on dough; cut around pattern with sharp knife. Repeat with remaining dough and scraps to make 12 bats.

6. Place cutouts on ungreased cookie sheets; sprinkle with cinnamon-sugar. Bake 8 to 10 minutes or until firm and edges are lightly browned. Cool on cookie sheets 3 minutes. Remove to wire rack; cool completely.

7. To decorate, pipe chocolate icing onto bats; pipe red icing onto balls for seams. *Makes 2 dozen cookies*

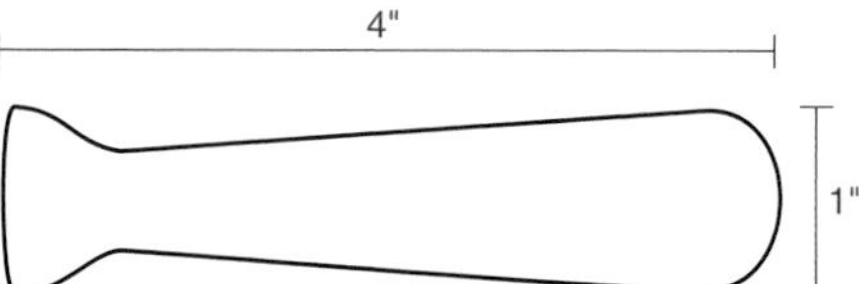

Snickerdoodle Batter-Ups

Bulls-Eyes

1 package (18 ounces) refrigerated sugar cookie dough
Black and red food colorings

1. Remove dough from wrapper. Divide dough in half; place in separate medium bowls. Let dough stand at room temperature about 15 minutes.

2. Add black food coloring to dough in one bowl and red food coloring to dough in remaining bowl. Beat doughs separately until evenly colored. Wrap doughs separately in plastic wrap; refrigerate 1 hour.

3. Preheat oven to 350°F. Roll black dough on lightly floured waxed paper to ¼-inch thickness. Sprinkle dough with flour to minimize sticking, if necessary. Cut dough using 3-inch round cookie cutter; place cutouts 2 inches apart on ungreased cookie sheets. Repeat with red dough, cutting out same number of red circles as black circles.

4. Cut and remove circles from centers of 3-inch cutouts using 2-inch round cookie cutter. Place red 2-inch circles into centers of black 3-inch rings; place black 2-inch circles into centers of red 3-inch rings.

5. Cut and remove circles from centers of 2-inch cutouts using 1-inch round cookie cutter. Place red 1-inch circles into centers of black 2-inch rings; place black 1-inch circles into centers of red 2-inch rings.

6. Bake 8 to 11 minutes or until firm but not browned. Cool on cookie sheets 10 minutes. Remove to wire rack; cool completely.

Makes about 1½ dozen cookies

Tie-Dyed T-Shirts

1 package (18 ounces) refrigerated sugar cookie dough
6 tablespoons all-purpose flour, divided
Red, yellow and blue food colorings

1. Preheat oven to 350°F. Grease cookie sheets.

2. Remove dough from wrapper. Divide into 3 pieces; place in separate medium bowls. Let dough stand at room temperature about 15 minutes.

3. Add 2 tablespoons flour and red food coloring to dough in one bowl; beat at medium speed of electric mixer until well blended and evenly colored. Wrap in plastic wrap; refrigerate 20 minutes. Repeat with second dough piece, 2 tablespoons flour and yellow food coloring. Repeat with remaining dough piece, remaining 2 tablespoons flour and blue food coloring.

4. Divide each color in half. Press together half of yellow dough with half of red dough. Roll dough on lightly floured surface to ¼-inch thickness. Cut dough with 3-inch T-shirt-shaped cookie cutter or make pattern (see Note). Place cutouts 2 inches apart on prepared cookie sheets. Repeat with remaining dough, pairing remaining yellow dough with half of blue dough and remaining red dough with remaining blue dough.

5. Bake 7 to 9 minutes or until firm but not browned. Cool completely on cookie sheets.

Makes about 1½ dozen cookies

Note: Using the photo as a guide, draw the pattern on clean, lightweight cardboard. Cut out the pattern and lightly spray one side with nonstick cooking spray. Place the pattern, sprayed side down, on rolled out dough; cut around it with a sharp knife.

Tic-Tac-Toe Cookies

- ¾ cup (1½ sticks) butter, softened
- ¾ cup granulated sugar
- 1 egg
- 1 teaspoon vanilla extract
- 2¼ cups all-purpose flour
- ½ teaspoon baking powder
- ¼ teaspoon salt
- 4 squares (1 ounce each) semi-sweet chocolate, melted
- ¼ cup powdered sugar
- 1 teaspoon water
- ½ cup "M&M's"® Chocolate Mini Baking Bits

In bowl cream butter and granulated sugar until light and fluffy; beat in egg and vanilla. In bowl mix flour, baking powder and salt; blend into creamed mixture. Reserve half of dough. Stir chocolate into remaining dough. Wrap; refrigerate doughs 30 minutes. Working with 1 dough at a time on lightly floured surface, roll or pat into 7×4½-inch rectangle. Cut dough into 9 (7×½-inch) strips. Repeat with remaining dough. Place 1 strip chocolate dough on sheet of plastic wrap. Place 1 strip vanilla dough next to chocolate dough. Place second strip of chocolate dough next to vanilla dough to make bottom layer. Prepare second row by stacking strips on first row, alternating vanilla dough over chocolate, and chocolate dough over vanilla. Repeat with third row to complete 1 bar. Repeat entire process with remaining dough strips, starting with vanilla dough, to complete second bar. Wrap both bars and refrigerate 1 hour. Preheat oven to 350°F. Grease cookie sheets. Cut bars crosswise into ¼-inch slices. Place 2 inches apart on prepared cookie sheets. Bake 10 to 12 minutes. Cool on cookie sheets 2 minutes; cool completely on wire racks. In bowl mix powdered sugar and water until smooth. Using icing to attach, decorate cookies with "M&M's"® Chocolate Mini Baking Bits to look like Tic-Tac-Toe games. *Makes 4 dozen cookies*

Ice Skates

½ cup (1 stick) butter, softened
1¼ cups honey
1 cup packed light brown sugar
1 egg, separated
5½ cups self-rising flour
1 teaspoon ground ginger
1 teaspoon ground cinnamon
½ cup milk
Prepared colored icings, sprinkles and small candy canes

1. Beat butter, honey, brown sugar and egg yolk in large bowl at medium speed of electric mixer until light and fluffy.

2. Combine flour, ginger and cinnamon in small bowl. Add alternately with milk to butter mixture; beat just until combined. Wrap in plastic wrap; refrigerate 30 minutes.

3. Preheat oven to 350°F. Grease cookie sheets.

4. Roll dough on lightly floured surface to ¼-inch thickness. Cut dough using 3½-inch boot-shaped cookie cutter or make pattern (see Note on page 218). Place cutouts 2 inches apart on prepared cookie sheets.

5. Bake 8 to 10 minutes or until edges are lightly browned. Cool on cookie sheets 2 minutes. Remove to wire racks; cool completely.

6. Decorate cookies with colored icings and sprinkles to look like ice skates, attaching candy canes as skate blades.

Makes about 4 dozen cookies

Journey to the Land of Make-Believe

Sparkling Magic Wands

1 package (18 ounces) refrigerated sugar cookie dough
48 pretzel sticks (2½ inches long)
Prepared colored icings
Colored sugar or edible glitter and gold dragées

1. Preheat oven to 350°F. Remove dough from wrapper.

2. Roll dough to ⅛-inch thickness on well-floured surface. Cut dough with 2-inch star-shaped cookie cutter. Place each star on top of 1 pretzel stick; press lightly to attach. Place on ungreased cookie sheet.

3. Bake 4 to 6 minutes or until edges are lightly browned. Carefully remove to wire racks; cool completely.

4. Spread icing on stars; sprinkle with colored sugar. Press dragées into points of stars. Let stand until set.

Makes 4 dozen cookies

Peanut Butter Aliens

1 package (18 ounces) refrigerated sugar cookie dough
½ cup creamy peanut butter
⅓ cup all-purpose flour
¼ cup powdered sugar
½ teaspoon vanilla
1 cup strawberry jam
Green decorating icing

1. Preheat oven to 350°F. Grease 2 cookie sheets. Remove dough from wrapper; place in large bowl. Let dough stand at room temperature about 15 minutes.

2. Add peanut butter, flour, powdered sugar and vanilla to dough; beat at medium speed of electric mixer until well blended. Divide dough in half; wrap 1 half in plastic wrap and refrigerate.

3. Roll remaining dough half to ¼-inch thickness on lightly floured surface. Cut into 14 (3-inch) rounds; pinch 1 side of each circle to make teardrop shape. Place cutouts 2 inches apart on prepared cookie sheets. Bake 12 to 14 minutes or until firm and lightly browned. Cool on cookie sheets 2 to 3 minutes. Remove to wire rack; cool completely.

4. Roll remaining dough to ¼-inch thickness on lightly floured surface. Cut into 14 (3-inch) rounds; pinch 1 side of each circle to make teardrop shape. Place cutouts 2 inches apart on prepared cookie sheets. Using sharp knife or mini cookie cutter, cut 2 oblong holes for eyes. Make small slit or third hole for mouth, if desired. Bake 12 to 14 minutes or until firm and lightly browned. Cool on cookie sheets 2 to 3 minutes. Remove to wire rack; cool completely.

5. Spread green icing on cookies with faces; let stand 10 minutes or until set. Spread about 1 tablespoon jam on each uncut cookie. To assemble, cover each jam-topped cookie with green face cookie. *Makes 14 sandwich cookies*

Tea Party Cookies

1 package (18 ounces) refrigerated sugar cookie dough
¼ cup all-purpose flour
1 teaspoon apple pie spice*
Almond Royal Icing (page 232)
Assorted food colorings, candy fruit slices and assorted decors and sprinkles

*Substitute ½ teaspoon ground cinnamon, ¼ teaspoon ground nutmeg and ⅛ teaspoon ground allspice or ground cloves for 1 teaspoon apple pie spice.

1. Preheat oven to 350°F. Grease 6 (3-inch) muffin pan cups. Remove dough from wrapper; place in large bowl. Let dough stand at room temperature about 15 minutes.

2. Add flour and apple pie spice to dough; beat until well blended. Divide dough in half. Wrap 1 half in plastic wrap; refrigerate until needed.

3. For cups, shape remaining dough into 6 balls; press onto bottoms and up sides of muffin cups. Freeze 10 minutes.

4. Bake cups 8 minutes. Immediately press back of floured round measuring spoon against sides and bottoms of cups to reshape. Bake 5 to 7 minutes; reshape, if necessary. Cool in pan 3 minutes. Remove to wire rack; cool completely.

5. For saucers, shape remaining dough into 6 (3-inch) discs. Place 2 inches apart on ungreased cookie sheets. Bake 7 minutes or until edges are lightly browned. Press down centers. Cool on cookie sheets 3 minutes. Remove to wire rack; cool completely.

6. Prepare Almond Royal Icing; spread on insides of cups. Let stand until set. Keep remaining icing tightly covered.

7. Tint remaining icing desired colors. With icing, attach 1 fruit slice to each cup for handle. Decorate as desired. Let stand 30 minutes or until set. To serve, place teacup cookies on saucer cookies. *Makes 6 teacup and saucer cookies*

Smilin' Cookies

1 package (18 ounces) refrigerated sugar cookie dough
4 teaspoons finely grated lemon peel
Yellow food coloring and yellow crystal sugar
¼ cup semisweet or milk chocolate chips

1. Remove dough from wrapper; place in large bowl. Let dough stand at room temperature about 15 minutes.

2. Add lemon peel and food coloring to dough; beat at medium speed of electric mixer until well blended and evenly colored. Wrap dough in plastic wrap; freeze 30 minutes.

3. Preheat oven to 350°F. Shape dough into 32 balls. Place 2 inches apart on ungreased cookie sheets; flatten into 1¾-inch rounds. Sprinkle with yellow sugar.

4. Bake 9 to 11 minutes or until set. Cool on cookie sheets 2 minutes. Remove to wire rack; cool completely.

5. Place chocolate chips in small resealable food storage bag; seal. Microwave on HIGH 1 minute; knead bag lightly. Microwave on HIGH for additional 30-second intervals until chips are completely melted, kneading bag after each interval. Cut off tiny corner of bag. Pipe chocolate onto cookies for eyes and mouths.

Makes 32 cookies

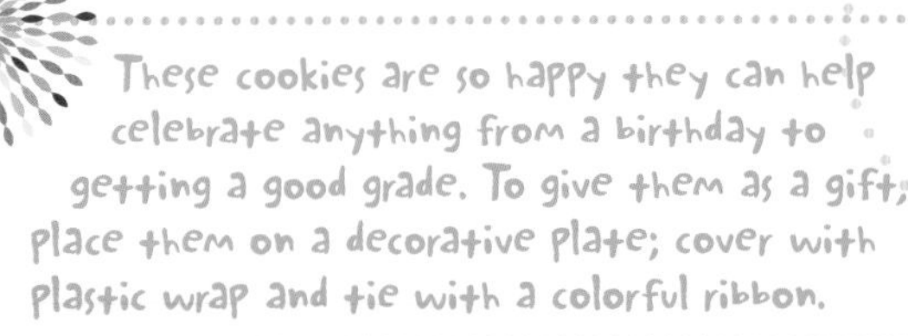

Cookie Necklaces

1 package (18 ounces) refrigerated sugar cookie dough
2 tablespoons all-purpose flour
1 tablespoon unsweetened Dutch process cocoa powder
Drinking straw
Almond Royal Icing (recipe follows) and colored sugars
Assorted food colorings and ¼-inch-wide curling ribbons in assorted colors, cut into lengths of 30 to 36 inches

1. Preheat oven to 350°F. Remove dough from wrapper; place in large bowl. Let dough stand at room temperature 15 minutes.

2. Add flour and cocoa to dough; beat until well blended. Divide dough into 4 equal pieces; wrap individually in plastic wrap and refrigerate 30 minutes.

3. Roll 1 dough piece on floured surface to ¼-inch thickness. Cut dough using 1- to 1½-inch cookie cutters. Place cutouts 2 inches apart on ungreased cookie sheets; make hole in center of each using straw. Repeat with remaining dough.

4. Bake 5 to 7 minutes or until firm but not browned. Make hole in center of each cutout again, if necessary. Cool on cookie sheets 2 minutes. Remove to wire rack; cool completely.

5. Prepare Almond Royal Icing; tint with food colorings as desired. Dip cookies into icings. Sprinkle with colored sugar. Let stand 40 minutes or until set.

6. Place 2 different color ribbons side by side; thread 9 or 10 cookies onto each. Knot ribbons together at ends.

Makes about 100 miniature cookies (enough for 10 necklaces)

Almond Royal Icing: Beat 2 egg whites (use only grade A, clean uncracked eggs) at high speed of electric mixer until foamy. Add 4 cups powdered sugar and ¾ teaspoon almond extract. Beat at low speed until moistened. Beat at high speed until icing is stiff; add additional powdered sugar if needed.

Cookie Necklace

Goofy Gus

1 package (18 ounces) refrigerated sugar cookie dough
1 egg yolk
¼ teaspoon water
Red food coloring
Prepared white frosting
10 packages (2 cakes each) coconut and marshmallow covered, snowball-shaped cakes
Assorted candies and tinted shredded coconut

1. Preheat oven to 350°F. Remove dough from wrapper.

2. Roll dough to ⅛-inch thickness on well-floured surface. Cut with 2¼-inch foot-shaped cookie cutter. Place cutouts 2 inches apart on ungreased cookie sheets, turning half of cookies over to make both left and right feet.

3. Combine egg yolk, water and food coloring in small bowl; stir until well blended. Using small, clean craft paintbrush, paint egg yolk mixture on feet to make toenails.

4. Bake 5 to 8 minutes or until golden brown. Remove to wire rack; cool completely.

5. Using small amount of frosting, attach 1 right and 1 left foot to each snowball cake. Decorate with assorted candies and coconut as desired. *Makes 20 desserts*

Coconut Craters

1 package (18 ounces) refrigerated chocolate chip cookie dough
¼ cup packed light brown sugar
2 tablespoons milk
1 tablespoon butter or margarine, melted
1 cup flaked coconut
½ cup chocolate-covered toffee baking pieces

1. Preheat oven to 350°F. Line 36 mini (1¾-inch) muffin pan cups with paper baking cups.

2. Remove dough from wrapper. Shape dough into 36 balls; press onto bottoms and up sides of muffin cups. Bake 9 to 11 minutes or until golden brown.

3. Meanwhile, combine brown sugar, milk and butter in medium bowl. Stir in coconut and toffee pieces. Gently press down center of each cookie with back of teaspoon. Spoon 1 rounded teaspoon toffee mixture into each cup. Bake 2 to 4 minutes or until golden. Cool in pan 10 minutes. Remove to wire rack; cool completely. *Makes 3 dozen cookies*

Masquerade Party Cookies

1 package (18 ounces) refrigerated chocolate chip cookie dough
¼ cup all-purpose flour
Colored nonpareils or sprinkles
Prepared black frosting
Red string licorice, cut into 5-inch lengths

1. Preheat oven to 350°F. Lightly grease cookie sheets. Remove dough from wrapper; place in large bowl. Let dough stand at room temperature about 15 minutes.

2. Add flour to dough; beat at medium speed of electric mixer until well blended.

3. Shape dough into 20 (3-inch long) ovals; roll in nonpareils. Place 2 inches apart on prepared cookie sheets; flatten slightly. Pinch ovals in at centers to create mask shapes. Decorate with additional nonpareils.

4. Bake 8 to 10 minutes or until edges are lightly browned. Make oval indentations for eyes with back of spoon. Reshape at centers, if necessary. Cool completely on cookie sheets.

5. Spread eye area with black frosting. Attach licorice piece to each side of mask with additional frosting. Let stand until frosting is set.

Makes 20 cookies

Adventures in the Animal Kingdom

Animal Pawprints

1 package (18 ounces) refrigerated sugar cookie dough
¼ cup unsweetened cocoa powder
Regular-sized and mini peanut butter chips

1. Preheat oven to 350°F. Grease cookie sheets.

2. Remove dough from wrapper; place in large bowl. Let dough stand at room temperature about 15 minutes.

3. Add cocoa to dough; beat at medium speed of electric mixer until well blended. For each cookie, shape 1 (1-inch) ball and 4 smaller balls. Place large ball on prepared cookie sheet; place small balls on one side of large ball.

4. Bake 12 to 14 minutes or until cookies are set and no longer shiny. Remove from oven; immediately place regular-sized peanut butter chip on first "toe" and place mini peanut butter chips on remaining "toes" of each cookie. Remove to wire rack; cool completely. *Makes 1½ dozen cookies*

Fido's Favorite Things

1 package (18 ounces) refrigerated oatmeal raisin cookie dough in squares or rounds (12 count)
Prepared colored icings
Colored sugars
Coarsely chopped pretzel sticks

1. Preheat oven to 350°F. Lightly grease cookie sheets.

2. Remove dough from wrapper; let stand at room temperature about 15 minutes.

3. For bone, with floured hands, shape dough square or round into 3½-inch-long rectangle. Make indentations in ends to resemble dog bone.* For food dish, pat dough square or round into 2-inch square; taper top to 1¾ inches and flare bottom to 3 inches. For fire hydrant, shape dough square or round into 2×1-inch fire hydrant shape.* Place dough shapes 2 inches apart on prepared cookie sheets.

4. Bake 13 to 15 minutes or until edges are lightly browned. Cool on cookie sheets 5 minutes. Remove to wire rack; cool completely.

5. Decorate with icings, sugars and pretzels as desired.

Makes 1 dozen cookies

*Or flatten dough with floured hands or rolling pin and cut with 2- to 3-inch cookie cutters.

Dino-Mite Dinosaurs

1 cup (2 sticks) butter, softened
1¼ cups granulated sugar
1 egg
2 squares (1 ounce each) semi-sweet chocolate, melted
½ teaspoon vanilla extract
2⅓ cups all-purpose flour
1 teaspoon baking powder
¼ teaspoon salt
1 cup white frosting
Assorted food colorings
1 cup "M&M's"® Chocolate Mini Baking Bits

In large bowl cream butter and sugar until light and fluffy; beat in egg, chocolate and vanilla. In medium bowl combine flour, baking powder and salt; add to creamed mixture. Wrap and refrigerate dough 2 to 3 hours. Preheat oven to 350°F. Working with half the dough at a time on lightly floured surface, roll to ¼-inch thickness. Cut into dinosaur shapes using 4-inch cookie cutters. Place about 2 inches apart on ungreased cookie sheets. Bake 10 to 12 minutes. Cool 2 minutes on cookie sheets; cool completely on wire racks. Tint frosting desired colors. Frost cookies and decorate with "M&M's"® Chocolate Mini Baking Bits. Store in tightly covered container.

Makes 2 dozen cookies

Luscious Lions

Manes

1 package (18 ounces) refrigerated sugar cookie dough
¼ cup all-purpose flour
2 tablespoons powdered sugar
Grated peel of 1 large orange
¼ teaspoon yellow gel food coloring
¼ teaspoon red gel food coloring

Faces

½ (18-ounce) package refrigerated sugar cookie dough*
2 tablespoons all-purpose flour
1 tablespoon powdered sugar
Grated peel of 1 lemon
¼ teaspoon yellow gel food coloring
Mini candy-coated chocolate pieces
Prepared white icing
Assorted decors
Prepared chocolate icing or melted chocolate

*Save remaining ½ package of dough for another use.

1. Grease 2 cookie sheets. For manes, remove 1 package dough from wrapper; place in large bowl. Let dough stand at room temperature about 15 minutes.

2. Add flour, powdered sugar, orange peel, yellow food coloring and red food coloring to dough; beat at medium speed of electric mixer until well blended and evenly colored. Shape into 24 large balls. Place 12 balls on each cookie sheet. Flatten balls into circles about 2¾ inches in diameter. Cut each circle with fluted 2½-inch round cookie cutter. Remove scraps and discard. Refrigerate 30 minutes.

continued on page 248

Luscious Lions, continued

3. Preheat oven to 350°F. Bake manes 12 to 14 minutes or until edges are lightly browned. Cool on cookie sheets 2 to 3 minutes. Remove to wire rack; cool completely.

4. For faces, remove ½ package of dough from wrapper; place in medium bowl. Let dough stand at room temperature about 15 minutes.

5. Add flour, powdered sugar, lemon peel and yellow food coloring to dough; beat at medium speed of electric mixer until well blended and evenly colored. Shape into 24 balls. Place on prepared cookie sheets. Flatten balls to slightly larger than 1½ inches in diameter. Cut into circles using smooth 1½-inch round cookie cutter. Remove scraps; shape into balls for ears. Attach 2 ears to each face. Place 2 candy pieces in center of each ear and place 1 candy piece for nose.

6. Bake 14 minutes or until edges are lightly browned. Cool on cookie sheets 2 to 3 minutes. Remove to wire rack; cool completely.

7. To assemble lions, attach faces to manes with icing. Pipe white icing onto faces and press decors into icing for eyes. Pipe chocolate icing onto faces for whiskers.

Makes 2 dozen cookies

Use the remaining half package of refrigerated sugar cookie dough to make lioness cookies! Simply follow the recipe and directions for making the lion faces, but after baking, do not attach them to manes.

Go Fish

½ cup (1 stick) butter, softened
¾ cup granulated sugar
¼ cup firmly packed light brown sugar
1 egg
1 egg white
½ teaspoon vanilla extract
2 cups all-purpose flour
1¼ teaspoons ground cinnamon
1 teaspoon baking powder
1 cup white frosting
Assorted food colorings
1 cup "M&M's"® Chocolate Mini Baking Bits

In large bowl cream butter and sugars until light and fluffy; beat in egg, egg white and vanilla. In medium bowl combine flour, cinnamon and baking powder; add to creamed mixture. Wrap and refrigerate dough 2 to 3 hours. Preheat oven to 325°F. Working with half the dough at a time on lightly floured surface, roll to ¼-inch thickness. Cut into fish shapes using 3-inch cookie cutters. Place about 2 inches apart on ungreased cookie sheets. Bake 10 to 12 minutes. Cool 2 minutes on cookie sheets; cool completely on wire racks. Tint frosting desired colors. Frost cookies and decorate with "M&M's"® Chocolate Mini Baking Bits. Store in tightly covered container. *Makes 2½ dozen cookies*

Chocolate Tortoises

1 package (18 ounces) refrigerated sugar cookie dough
⅓ cup unsweetened cocoa powder
1 tablespoon powdered sugar
½ teaspoon vanilla
30 caramels, unwrapped
Pecan halves
½ cup (3 ounces) semisweet chocolate chips
Silver dragées or decors

1. Preheat oven to 350°F. Grease 30 mini (1¾-inch) muffin pan cups. Remove dough from wrapper; place in large bowl. Let dough stand at room temperature about 15 minutes.

2. Add cocoa, powdered sugar and vanilla to dough; beat at medium speed of electric mixer until well blended.

3. Shape dough into 30 balls; press onto bottoms and up sides of muffin cups. Bake 10 minutes. Press 1 caramel into each chocolate cup. Return to oven 2 to 3 minutes or until caramels are soft. Working quickly, press 5 pecans into caramel for legs and head. Let cool in pan 5 minutes. Remove to wire rack; cool completely.

4. Place wire rack over waxed paper. Place chocolate chips in small microwavable bowl. Microwave on HIGH 1 to 1½ minutes. Stir after 1 minute and on 30-second intervals after first minute until chips are melted and smooth. Attach 2 silver dragées to head with chocolate for eyes. Drizzle remaining chocolate over tops of tortoises as desired. Let stand until chocolate is completely set.

Makes 2½ dozen cookies

Chocolate Tortoises

Spiky Hedgehogs

1 package (18 ounces) refrigerated chocolate chip cookie dough with caramel filling in squares or rounds (20 count)
½ cup uncooked quick or old-fashioned oats
½ cup all-purpose flour
2½ packages (1.5 ounces each) chocolate-covered crisp wafer candy bars, separated into sticks
⅔ cup creamy peanut butter
2 tablespoons butter or margarine
1 cup powdered sugar
½ teaspoon vanilla
2 to 3 tablespoons milk
1 cup toasted coconut
Mini chocolate chips

1. Grease cookie sheets. Remove dough from wrapper; place in large bowl. Let dough stand at room temperature 15 minutes. Add oats and flour to dough; beat until well blended.

2. Preheat oven to 350°F. Cut candy sticks in half crosswise to make 20 pieces. Divide dough into 20 pieces. Wrap dough pieces around candy pieces, completely covering tops and sides. Place 2 inches apart on prepared cookie sheets; pinch 1 end of dough to make pointy. Freeze 10 minutes or until firm.

3. Bake cookies 10 to 12 minutes or until firm and edges are lightly browned. Cool on cookie sheets 2 minutes. Remove to wire rack; cool completely.

4. Beat peanut butter and butter until well blended. Stir in powdered sugar and vanilla. Add milk by tablespoons until of desired frosting consistency. Reserve 1 tablespoon frosting.

5. Frost cookie tops and sides with remaining frosting, leaving pointed ends unfrosted. Place coconut in bowl. Dip frosted ends of cookies into coconut to cover. Using reserved frosting, attach chocolate chips for eyes and noses on pointed ends of cookies.

Makes 20 cookies

Octo-Cookies

1 package (18 ounces) refrigerated chocolate chip cookie dough
¼ cup all-purpose flour
10 whole almonds (or 10 walnut or pecan halves)
Powdered Sugar Glaze (page 256)
Assorted food colorings
Prepared colored icings and candies

1. Preheat oven to 350°F. Grease 10 mini (1¾-inch) muffin pan cups. Remove dough from wrapper; place in large bowl. Let dough stand at room temperature about 15 minutes.

2. Add flour to dough; beat at medium speed of electric mixer until well blended. Reserve ⅓ of dough. Wrap remaining ⅔ of dough in plastic wrap; refrigerate.

3. For heads, divide reserved ⅓ dough into 10 equal pieces. Place almond in center of each piece; shape into balls, covering nut completely. Place balls in prepared muffin cups. Freeze 10 minutes. Bake 10 minutes or just until firm. Gently loosen cookies around edges with tip of small knife or metal spatula. Cool in pan 10 minutes. Remove to wire rack; cool completely.

4. For legs, divide remaining dough into 10 equal portions. Divide each portion into 8 pieces; shape each piece into ropes of varying lengths from 1½ to 2 inches long. Shape tips at one end to a point. Arrange 8 legs with thicker end of legs touching in center and pointed ends about ¼ inch away from each other at outside of circular shape. Bake 6 to 8 minutes or just until legs are firm. Cool completely on cookie sheets.

continued on page 256

Octo-Cookies, continued

5. Place wire racks over waxed paper. Carefully transfer legs to wire racks. Prepare Powdered Sugar Glaze; tint glaze with food colorings as desired.

6. Attach heads to legs using glaze; let stand 15 minutes or until set. Spread remaining glaze over cookies. Let stand about 40 minutes or until completely set.

7. Outline legs and decorate faces with icings and candies as desired.

Makes 10 large cookies

Powdered Sugar Glaze

2 cups powdered sugar
7 to 9 tablespoons heavy cream, divided

1. Combine powdered sugar and 6 tablespoons cream in medium bowl; whisk until smooth.

2. Add enough remaining cream, 1 tablespoon at a time, to make medium-thick pourable glaze.

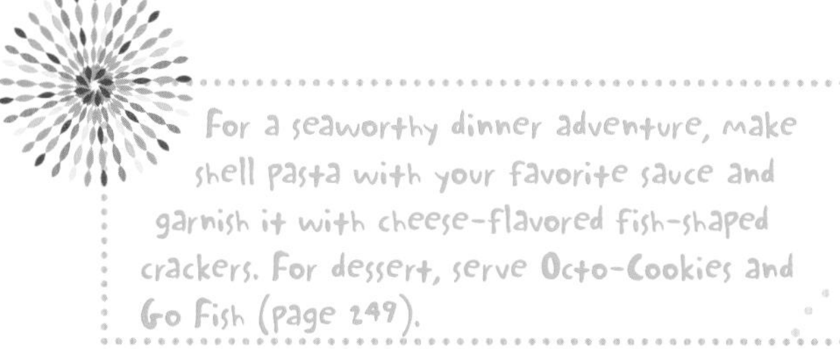

Monkey Bars

3 cups miniature marshmallows
½ cup honey
⅓ cup butter
¼ cup peanut butter
2 teaspoons vanilla
¼ teaspoon salt
4 cups crispy rice cereal
2 cups rolled oats, uncooked
½ cup flaked coconut
¼ cup peanuts

Combine marshmallows, honey, butter, peanut butter, vanilla and salt in medium saucepan. Melt marshmallow mixture over low heat, stirring constantly. Combine rice cereal, oats, coconut and peanuts in 13×9×2-inch baking pan. Pour marshmallow mixture over dry ingredients. Mix until thoroughly coated. Press mixture firmly into pan. Cool completely before cutting. *Makes 2 dozen bars*

Microwave Directions: Microwave marshmallows, honey, butter, peanut butter, vanilla and salt in 2-quart microwave-safe bowl on HIGH 2½ to 3 minutes. Continue as directed above.

Favorite recipe from ***National Honey Board***

Czech Bear Paws

4 cups ground toasted hazelnuts
2 cups all-purpose flour
1 tablespoon unsweetened cocoa powder
1 teaspoon ground cinnamon
½ teaspoon ground nutmeg
¼ teaspoon salt
1 cup (2 sticks) plus 3 teaspoons butter, softened, divided
1 cup powdered sugar
1 egg yolk
½ cup chocolate chips, melted
Slivered almonds, halved

1. Preheat oven to 350°F. Combine hazelnuts, flour, cocoa, cinnamon, nutmeg and salt in medium bowl.

2. Beat 1 cup butter, powdered sugar and egg yolk in large bowl until light and fluffy. Gradually add flour mixture. Beat until soft dough forms.

3. Grease 3 madeleine pans with remaining butter, 1 teaspoon per pan; dust with flour. (If only 1 pan is available, thoroughly wash, dry, regrease and flour after baking each batch. Cover remaining dough with plastic wrap; stand at room temperature.) Press level tablespoonfuls of dough into each mold.

4. Bake 12 minutes or until centers are set. Let stand in pan 3 minutes. Loosen cookies from pan with point of small knife. Invert pan over wire rack; tap lightly to release cookies. Let stand 2 minutes. Cool completely, shell side up.

5. Pipe melted chocolate onto curved end of each cookie; place slivered almonds halves in melted chocolate for claws. Let stand at room temperature 1 hour or until set.

6. Store tightly covered at room temperature.

Makes about 5 dozen cookies

Note: These cookies do not freeze well.

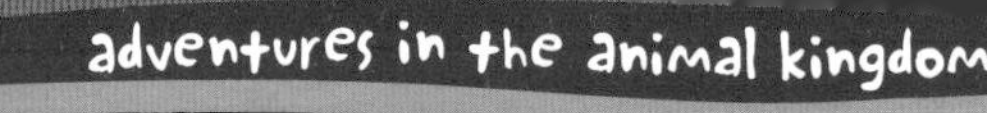

Peppermint Pigs

1 package (18 ounces) refrigerated sugar cookie dough
½ cup all-purpose flour
¾ teaspoon peppermint extract
Red food coloring
Prepared white icing and mini candy-coated chocolate pieces

1. Preheat oven to 350°F. Lightly grease cookie sheets.

2. Remove dough from wrapper; place in large bowl. Let dough stand at room temperature about 15 minutes.

3. Add flour, peppermint extract and food coloring to dough; beat at medium speed of electric mixer until well blended and evenly colored. Divide dough into 20 equal pieces.

4. For each pig, shape 1 dough piece into 1 (1-inch) ball, 1 (½-inch) ball and 2 (¼-inch) balls. Flatten 1-inch ball to ¼-inch-thick round; place on prepared cookie sheet. Flatten ½-inch ball to ¼-inch-thick oval; place on top of dough round for snout. Shape 2 (¼-inch) balls into triangles; fold point over and place at top of round for ears. Make indentations in snout with wooden skewer for nostrils.

5. Bake 9 to 11 minutes or until set. Remove to wire racks; cool completely. Use white icing and candy-coated chocolate pieces to make eyes. *Makes 20 cookies*

Peanut Butter Critter Cookies

3 cups all-purpose flour
1 cup (2 sticks) butter, softened
1 cup peanut butter chips, melted
¾ cup granulated sugar
¼ cup packed brown sugar
1 egg
1½ teaspoons milk
1 teaspoon vanilla
Powdered sugar
Prepared colored icings

1. Combine flour, butter, melted peanut butter chips, granulated sugar, brown sugar, egg, milk and vanilla in large bowl. Beat at low speed of electric mixer 1 to 2 minutes, scraping bowl often, until well blended. Divide dough in half. Wrap in plastic wrap; refrigerate 1 to 2 hours or until firm.

2. Preheat oven to 375°F. Roll out dough on well-floured surface to ⅛-inch thickness. Cut desired shapes using 2½-inch cookie cutters. Place 1 inch apart on ungreased cookie sheets.

3. Bake 5 to 8 minutes or until edges are lightly browned. Remove immediately to wire racks; cool completely. Sprinkle with powdered sugar or decorate with icings as desired.

Makes about 4 dozen cookies

Celebrating the Holidays

Springtime Nests

1 cup butterscotch chips
½ cup light corn syrup
½ cup creamy peanut butter
⅓ cup sugar
2½ cups chow mein noodles
2 cups cornflakes, lightly crushed
Jelly beans or malted milk egg candies

1. Combine butterscotch chips, corn syrup, peanut butter and sugar in large microwavable bowl. Microwave on HIGH 1 to 1½ minutes or until melted and smooth, stirring at 30-second intervals.

2. Stir in chow mein noodles and cornflakes until evenly coated. Quickly shape scant ¼ cupfuls mixture into balls; make indentation in centers to make nests. Place nests on waxed paper to set. Place 3 jelly beans in each nest.

Makes 1½ dozen treats

Uncle Sam's Hat

1 package (18 ounces) refrigerated chocolate chip cookie dough
2 cups powdered sugar
2 to 4 tablespoons milk
Red and blue food colorings

1. Preheat oven to 350°F. Lightly grease 12-inch round pizza pan and cookie sheet. Remove dough from wrapper. Press dough evenly into prepared pizza pan. Cut dough into hat shape as shown in photo. Press scraps together and flatten heaping tablespoons dough onto prepared cookie sheet. Using 1½- to 2-inch star cookie cutter, cut out 3 stars; remove and discard dough scraps.

2. Bake stars 5 to 7 minutes and hat 7 to 9 minutes or until edges are lightly browned. Cool stars on cookie sheet 1 minute. Remove stars to wire rack; cool completely. Cool hat completely on pan on wire rack.

3. Combine powdered sugar and enough milk, 1 tablespoon at a time, to make medium-thick pourable glaze. Spread small amount of glaze over stars and place on waxed paper; let stand until glaze is set. Using red and blue food colorings, tint ½ of glaze red, tint ¼ of glaze blue and leave remaining ¼ of glaze white.

4. Decorate hat with red, white and blue glazes as shown in photo; place stars on blue band of hat. Let stand until glaze is set. *Makes 1 large cookie*

Smucker's® Spider Web Tartlets

1 (18-ounce) log refrigerated sugar cookie dough
¾ cup all-purpose flour
CRISCO® Nonstick Cooking Spray or parchment paper
1 cup (12-ounce jar) SMUCKER'S® Apricot Preserves
1 tube black decorating gel

1. Preheat oven to 375°F. Unwrap cookie dough and place in medium mixing bowl. With floured hands, knead flour into cookie dough. Roll dough back into log shape; place on clean cutting board and cut into eight equal slices. With floured fingers, place dough circles on baking sheet lined with parchment paper or sprayed with nonstick spray.

2. Gently press dough circles, flattening to make each one approximately 4 inches in diameter. With thumb and forefinger, pinch edge of each dough circle to create ridge all around. Pinch each dough circle along ridge to make eight points.

3. Spread 2 tablespoons SMUCKER'S® Preserves (or Simply Fruit) onto each dough circle, making sure to spread it all the way to edges and in each point. Refrigerate 20 minutes. Bake 12 to 14 minutes or until edges are lightly browned.

4. Remove tartlets from baking sheet and cool on wire rack. When cool, use black decorating gel to make spider web design.

Makes 8 servings

Gobbler Cookies

1 package (18 ounces) refrigerated sugar cookie dough
¼ cup all-purpose flour
2 teaspoons ground cinnamon
White, red, yellow and orange decorating icings
Chocolate sprinkles, mini chocolate chips and red licorice

1. Preheat oven to 350°F. Lightly grease cookie sheets. Remove dough from wrapper; place in large bowl. Let dough stand at room temperature about 15 minutes.

2. Add flour and cinnamon to dough; beat at medium speed of electric mixer until well blended.

3. Shape dough into 12 (1½-inch) balls, 12 (1-inch balls) and 12 (¾-inch) balls.

4. Flatten large balls into 4-inch rounds on prepared cookie sheets; freeze 10 minutes. Bake 9 to 11 minutes or until edges are lightly browned. Remove to wire rack; cool completely.

5. Flatten medium balls into 2¼-inch rounds on prepared cookie sheets; freeze 10 minutes. Bake 8 to 10 minutes or until edges are lightly browned. Remove to wire rack; cool completely.

6. Flatten small balls into 1-inch rounds on prepared cookie sheets; freeze 10 minutes. Bake 6 to 8 minutes or until edges are lightly browned. Remove to wire rack; cool completely.

7. Decorate large cookies with red, yellow and orange icings and chocolate sprinkles to make feathers. Place medium cookies on large cookies, towards bottom; place small cookies above medium cookies on large cookies. Decorate turkeys as shown in photo using icings, chocolate chips, chocolate sprinkles and licorice to make eyes, beaks, gobblers and feet. Let stand 20 minutes or until set.

Makes 1 dozen large cookies

Hanukkah Cookies

- ½ cup (1 stick) unsalted butter, softened
- 1 package (3 ounces) cream cheese, softened
- ½ cup sugar
- ¼ cup honey
- 1 egg
- ½ teaspoon vanilla
- 2½ cups all-purpose flour
- ⅓ cup finely ground walnuts
- 1 teaspoon baking powder
- ¼ teaspoon salt
- Prepared blue, white and yellow icings

1. Beat butter, cream cheese, sugar, honey, egg and vanilla in large bowl at medium speed of electric mixer until creamy. Stir in flour, walnuts, baking powder and salt until well blended. Shape dough into disc; wrap in plastic wrap. Refrigerate about 2 hours or until firm.

2. Preheat oven to 350°F. Lightly grease cookie sheets. Roll out dough, small portion at a time, to ¼-inch thickness on floured surface with lightly floured rolling pin. (Keep remaining dough wrapped in refrigerator until needed.) Cut dough with 2½-inch dreidel-shaped cookie cutter and 6-pointed star cookie cutter. Place 2 inches apart on prepared cookie sheets.

3. Bake 8 to 10 minutes or until edges are lightly browned. Let cookies stand on cookie sheets 1 to 2 minutes. Remove to wire racks; cool completely. Decorate cookies with icings as desired.

Makes 3½ dozen cookies

Fireside Cookie

1 package (18 ounces) refrigerated cookie dough, any flavor
Prepared icings and assorted candies

1. Preheat oven to 350°F. Line 2 large cookie sheets with parchment paper.

2. Remove dough from wrapper. Using about ¼ of dough, roll into 12×3-inch strip on lightly floured surface. Trim to 11×2¼ inches; set aside. Roll remaining dough into 10×8-inch rectangle. Trim to 9×7¾ inches; place on 1 prepared cookie sheet. Place reserved dough strip at top of rectangle to make fireplace mantel. Roll remaining scraps; cut into stocking shapes. Place on remaining prepared cookie sheet.

3. Bake 10 minutes or until edges are lightly browned. Cool on cookie sheets 5 minutes. Remove stocking cookies to wire rack. Slide large cookie and parchment paper onto wire rack; cool completely.

4. Decorate with icings and candies as shown, attaching stockings to fireplace cookie with icing.

Makes 1 large cookie

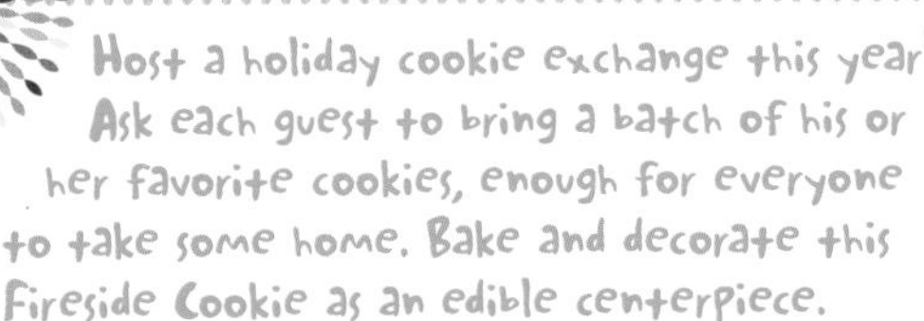

Valentine's Day Cookie Cards

Butter Cookie Dough (recipe follows)
1 container (16 ounces) vanilla frosting
1 container (16 ounces) pink cherry-flavored frosting
Assorted candies

Supplies
Pastry bags and assorted decorating tips

1. Prepare cookie dough. Cover; refrigerate about 4 hours or until firm.

2. Preheat oven to 350°F. Grease cookie sheets.

3. Roll out cookie dough to ⅛-inch thickness on lightly floured surface. Cut out 4½×3-inch rectangles. Place on prepared cookie sheets.

4. Bake 8 to 10 minutes or until edges are lightly browned. Remove to wire racks; cool completely.

5. Frost cookies with vanilla and cherry frostings; spoon remaining frostings into pastry bags fitted with decorating tips. Decorate cookies with frostings and candies as desired to resemble Valentine's Day cards. *Makes 1 dozen cookies*

Butter Cookie Dough

¾ cup (1½ sticks) butter, softened
¼ cup granulated sugar
¼ cup packed light brown sugar
1 egg yolk
1¾ cups all-purpose flour
¾ teaspoon baking powder
⅛ teaspoon salt

Combine butter, granulated sugar, brown sugar and egg yolk in medium bowl. Add flour, baking powder and salt; mix well.

You are too cool
All my Love
Mine

Shamrock Ice Cream Sandwiches

Butter Cookie Dough (page 276)
Green food coloring
1 pint ice cream or frozen yogurt, any flavor

1. Prepare cookie dough; tint desired shade of green with food coloring. Wrap in plastic wrap; refrigerate until firm, about 4 hours or overnight.

2. Preheat oven to 350°F.

3. Roll out dough on lightly floured surface to ¼-inch thickness. Cut dough using 3½- to 5-inch shamrock-shaped cookie cutter. Place on ungreased cookie sheets.

4. Bake 8 to 10 minutes or until edges are lightly browned. Remove to wire rack; cool completely.

5. Remove ice cream from freezer; let stand at room temperature to soften slightly, about 10 minutes. Spread 4 to 5 tablespoons ice cream onto flat sides of half the cookies. Place remaining cookies, flat sides down, on ice cream; press cookies together lightly.

6. Wrap each sandwich in aluminum foil or plastic wrap; freeze until firm, about 2 hours or overnight.

Makes 6 to 8 ice cream sandwich cookies

Note: Filled cookies store well up to 1 week in the freezer.

Acknowledgments

The publisher would like to thank the companies and organizations listed below for the use of their recipes and photographs in this publication.

California Dried Plum Board

California Tree Fruit Agreement

Cherry Marketing Institute

ConAgra Foods®

Dole Food Company, Inc.

Duncan Hines® and Moist Deluxe® are registered trademarks of Aurora Foods Inc.

Eagle Brand®

Hershey Foods Corporation

Keebler® Company

Lawry's® Foods

© Mars, Incorporated 2004

National Honey Board

The J.M. Smucker Company

Mott's® is a registered trademark of Mott's, LLP

Nestlé USA

Reckitt Benckiser Inc.

StarKist Seafood Company

Unilever

Washington Apple Commission

Index

D

E

METRIC CONVERSION CHART

VOLUME MEASUREMENTS (dry)

1/8 teaspoon = 0.5 mL
1/4 teaspoon = 1 mL
1/2 teaspoon = 2 mL
3/4 teaspoon = 4 mL
1 teaspoon = 5 mL
1 tablespoon = 15 mL
2 tablespoons = 30 mL
1/4 cup = 60 mL
1/3 cup = 75 mL
1/2 cup = 125 mL
2/3 cup = 150 mL
3/4 cup = 175 mL
1 cup = 250 mL
2 cups = 1 pint = 500 mL
3 cups = 750 mL
4 cups = 1 quart = 1 L

VOLUME MEASUREMENTS (fluid)

1 fluid ounce (2 tablespoons) = 30 mL
4 fluid ounces (1/2 cup) = 125 mL
8 fluid ounces (1 cup) = 250 mL
12 fluid ounces (1 1/2 cups) = 375 mL
16 fluid ounces (2 cups) = 500 mL

WEIGHTS (mass)

1/2 ounce = 15 g
1 ounce = 30 g
3 ounces = 90 g
4 ounces = 120 g
8 ounces = 225 g
10 ounces = 285 g
12 ounces = 360 g
16 ounces = 1 pound = 450 g

DIMENSIONS

1/16 inch = 2 mm
1/8 inch = 3 mm
1/4 inch = 6 mm
1/2 inch = 1.5 cm
3/4 inch = 2 cm
1 inch = 2.5 cm

OVEN TEMPERATURES

250°F = 120°C
275°F = 140°C
300°F = 150°C
325°F = 160°C
350°F = 180°C
375°F = 190°C
400°F = 200°C
425°F = 220°C
450°F = 230°C

BAKING PAN SIZES

Utensil	Size in Inches/Quarts	Metric Volume	Size in Centimeters
Baking or Cake Pan (square or rectangular)	8×8×2	2 L	20×20×5
	9×9×2	2.5 L	23×23×5
	12×8×2	3 L	30×20×5
	13×9×2	3.5 L	33×23×5
Loaf Pan	8×4×3	1.5 L	20×10×7
	9×5×3	2 L	23×13×7
Round Layer Cake Pan	8×1½	1.2 L	20×4
	9×1½	1.5 L	23×4
Pie Plate	8×1¼	750 mL	20×3
	9×1¼	1 L	23×3
Baking Dish or Casserole	1 quart	1 L	—
	1½ quart	1.5 L	—
	2 quart	2 L	—